Fredericksburg
Virginia

Fredericksburg

Virginia

Eclectic Histories
for the Curious Reader

TED KAMIENIAK

Charleston   London

History
PRESS

Published by The History Press
Charleston, SC 29403
www.historypress.net

Cover design by Marshall Hudson.

First published 2008

Manufactured in the United Kingdom

ISBN 978.1.59629.383.0

Library of Congress Cataloging-in-Publication Data

Kamieniak, Ted.
Fredericksburg, Virginia : eclectic histories for the curious reader / Ted Kamieniak.
p. cm.
ISBN-13: 978-1-59629-383-0 (alk. paper)
1. Fredericksburg (Va.)--History--Anecdotes. 2. Spotsylvania County
(Va.)--History--Anecdotes. I. Title.
F234.F8K36 2008
975.5'366--dc22
                          2007046017

Notice: The information in this book is true and complete to the best of our knowledge. It is offered without guarantee on the part of the author or The History Press. The author and The History Press disclaim all liability in connection with the use of this book.

To Robert A. Hodge

Contents

Preface

For the benefit of the reader unfamiliar with this area and its history, the city of Fredericksburg was established as a town in 1728 by the Virginia House of Burgesses. The General Assembly, then seated in Williamsburg, created Spotsylvania County in 1720. Spotsylvania's court met at Fredericksburg between 1732 and 1780. The histories of these two jurisdictions are inextricably intermingled.

Other counties proximal to Fredericksburg (Stafford, Caroline, King George and others) have always been tightly linked to this colonial port on the Rappahannock River as well. Fredericksburg meant *town* to the widespread occupants of the crossroads hamlets, plantations and isolated farmsteads throughout this region. That was true in the early eighteenth century and continued to be true as our nation's history unfolded.

It is true today as Fredericksburg is the cultural and historic heart of the region. The city and surrounding counties have an exceptional pedigree of place that the modern environment has injured but not extinguished. Many significant and beautiful places remain throughout this region. There is much here worth visiting. In my opinion the area retains a good deal of its small-town qualities, despite tremendous growth.

The articles contained herein were first published in Fredericksburg, Virginia, in the *Free Lance-Star*'s weekend magazine, *Town & County*. Topics were selected whimsically. I never set out to compile these articles, hence the varied and partially incongruous bundle of subject matter. The threads that bind these essays together are their relevance or connection to the Fredericksburg area and my inclination to write about overlooked themes and ordinary events in the history of human experiences.

It is worth emphasizing that Fredericksburg has a rich newspaper publishing tradition that began with the *Virginia Herald*, which published biweekly for about eighty-nine years starting in 1787, and continued up to the present-day *Free Lance-Star*, which was founded in September 1926 when the morning *Free Lance* was joined with the evening *Daily Star* to form a single publication that still serves the region so well today.

American history resonates in perpetuity. It constitutes fascinating adventure. It offers mystery, excitement, controversy, romance, ugliness, astonishment, sublime discovery, fulfillment and perhaps most importantly, invaluable pragmatic insight and guidance. Its study spawns an unending backlog of new interrogatives and investigative demands. It is a maze without exit. It will always have its unconquered frontiers because so much of the American saga is relegated to darkness. Only through painstaking examination is it possible for American civilization to scrutinize its past, to better understand what has been, comprehend what is now and visualize what may lie ahead. I encourage you to look.

Fredericksburg, Virginia
October 2, 2007

Acknowledgements

No writing project, even a modest one, emerges from solitary circumstances. I extend appreciation to those whose assistance I enjoyed and from which I benefited.

I dedicated this book to Mr. Robert A. Hodge, former resident of Fredericksburg and an educator at the high school and community college level. Time is the individual's most valuable possession. Mr. Hodge donated a great deal of his time to us. To the benefit of historians, researchers and genealogists he indexed all thirteen surviving historic newspapers published in Fredericksburg from 1787 to 1926. The resulting indices are of ineffable value, and will be for generations to come.

Gwen Woolf, editor of the *Free Lance-Star*'s *Town & County* magazine, has always graciously accepted my submissions and given to them her careful consideration. Her magazine, appearing each weekend, is a local favorite, being searched out first on Saturday mornings by more than a few loyal readers.

With the assistance of the faculty at the University of Mary Washington's Department of Historic Preservation, I believe I cultivated useful skills in researching, interpreting and chronicling history. I refer specifically to Professors Gary Stanton, John Pearce and Douglas W. Sanford, who introduced me to an abundance of fresh perspectives and investigative models, as well as an invigorating appreciation for the study of American civilization, culture and related disciplines. They are a dedicated and inspiring group of scholars.

Let me note that the people at the following repositories and institutions were always kind and knowledgeable about their collections—patient, professional and helpful without exception: the Library of Virginia; the Virginia Historical Society; the Simpson Library at the University of Mary

Washington; the Central Rappahannock Regional Library; the Central Rappahannock Heritage Center; the officials and personnel of the circuit courts of Fredericksburg and Spotsylvania; and others whose cooperation enabled me to speak with respondents and to access private property so that I might better understand aspects of this region's past.

I extend loving thanks to my wife Cindy and my daughter Eva for proofing many of my articles and providing useful criticism and happy encouragement.

The Little Castle

The Little Castle, located on Old Salem Church Road in northern Spotsylvania, is anything but commonplace. The man who erected this vernacular castle was determined to make his special mark on the landscape.

Its fanciful form was the creation of L.A. Vaughan. The present owner, Myrtle Carr, remembers the builder.

"He was a brick mason and a rock man. He built it himself," she said.

Circuit court records indicate that Vaughan purchased the property in 1950. Shortly thereafter he erected the house. Grover Rodgers has lived across the road for fifty-two years and remembers Vaughan declaring, "I'm gonna build one like nobody else."

The one-story, five-room house is clad in thin stone veneer. The perimeter of its flat roof is embellished with castellated parapets. Delicate decorative metalwork, in a motif of arches and arrows, fills the spaces between the parapets.

The tapering turret, rising above the roofline, is capped with a course of stone and a plain metal pinnacle. The turret is outfitted with a tiny illuminated window, creating the whimsical illusion of functional space within.

Old Salem Church Road is a short street, essentially one block long, near the intersection of Salem Church Road and State Route 3. Sixteen lots fronting it were created from an eight-acre tract, split off from the J.K. Dickenson farm and subdivided in 1937. Back then the artery was known as "the road leading from Orange Turnpike to White's Crossing," according to deed books.

The Little Castle is reminiscent of the fanciful roadside architecture that sprouted along America's thoroughfares in the 1920s and 1930s: diners

An oblique view of the Little Castle. The Little Castle, as it was known, was built by stonemason L.A. Vaughan in the early 1950s in northern Spotsylvania. It was demolished in 2004 to make way for a child-care business. *Courtesy of the author.*

in the shape of coffeepots; Long Island's Big Duck, from which poultry and eggs were sold; lunch counter businesses in the shape of hot dogs or tamales; and other commercial buildings whose shapes or façades were visual representations of goods or services sold within.

Intense competition for the motorist's dollar spurred ingenuity and imagination in designing increasingly dramatic and outlandish edifices to lure customers.

The Little Castle, being designed and built by a mason, may have been intended as an advertisement as well as a unique personal expression. Its unusual form would be effective in signaling the availability, skill and creativity of Vaughan.

California was the principal setting for this kind of building. It comes as no surprise that when Rodgers recalled Vaughan's source of inspiration for the Little Castle's design, he said, "He traveled a lot in California. He saw one like it in the desert there."

Myrtle Carr and her husband bought the place from Vaughan's heirs about thirty years ago.

When asked if she'd ever thought about remodeling the exterior to create a more conventional appearance, Carr replied, "Oh never. That's why we bought the house—we loved it!"

The Carrs did make some changes on the inside. She said the house originally had "too many cubbyholes."

Carr also pointed out an advantage to living in the Little Castle: "The delivery people always find you."

The Little Castle is a unique component of Spotsylvania County's architectural heritage. "Lots of people from out of state take pictures," said Carr.

She has put the house on the market because she is advanced in years and the place is too much for her to manage. Her husband, Woodrow Wilson Carr, died last April.

The house illustrates the unique ideas and intentions of its designer, builder and original occupant. It is meaningful and relevant to local history because of its distinctive physical characteristics. Its bold nonconformity and delightful idiosyncrasy constitute a visual treat.

Published August 28, 1998.

The Jail
of the County

To folks unfamiliar with the Historic Courthouse District in Spotsylvania, there is little indication that the beige, two-story, slate-roofed building, clad in stucco and located at the southwest corner of the courthouse green, served as the jail of the county for eighty-eight years. Iron that secured the building's openings was reportedly scrapped for war material soon after the jail was ordered closed in January 1943. The heavy board and batten door, visible in the photograph on pages 18–19, was discarded sometime after this image was recorded.

Generally, local Virginia jails erected in the antebellum period mirrored dwelling houses in plan and form. What distinguishes the building type are the materials and techniques applied to further improve security. Heavy masonry, walls, iron bars, sleepers (joists) closely spaced and cells lined with three-inch oak planks were essential specifications. The post-Revolutionary revisal of the penal codes decreased the frequency and variety of brutality (rooted in ancient legal principles of retribution in kind) used to punish criminals throughout the colonial period. As a consequence, local authorities' reliance on imprisonment in executing sentences increased. Tight containers for lawbreakers were an imperative, since the ability of local government to uphold the law depended on effective detention more so than before. A porous jail was in violation of the laws of the commonwealth, and could only lead to embarrassment and trouble for local officials. These bulky little buildings—often sited for enhanced public exposure in this period—reassured citizens that their safety was the government's concern. "No punishment, no government; no government, no political society," said the eighteenth-century English prison reformer and penitentiary designer Jeremy Bentham.

The façade of Spotsylvania's 1855 county jail. The jail was ordered closed in 1943. The building still stands on the courthouse green, having recently been refurbished by Spotsylvania Preservation Foundation Inc., a historic preservation group. This

image of the jail was created by the Historic American Buildings Survey in the 1930s. *Courtesy of the Library of Congress.*

Spotsylvania's seat of government was moved to its present site in 1839 from a two-acre tract on Blockhouse Road at the Po River. Lewis Rawlings conveyed ten acres to the court for the new county seat. He also built the first jail there, using material (bricks, iron and timber) from the old jail at the previous site. By nature of their function, jails were difficult to maintain—they were relentlessly battered, pried apart and picked at by restless, disgruntled and desperate prisoners. Maintenance cycles were intensive, with jail repair demanding frequent attention from the court. Certainly no other building type received such a pounding in the course of its intended use.

From the mid-1840s and on, numerous orders were recorded in which the court charged various commissioners with inspecting and reporting on the state of the jail, and with correcting deficiencies in security, sanitation and other problems. "The said jail having been recently broken by prisoners therein has been mended, but not securely," stated a report delivered to the court in 1846.

In February 1853 the jail burned. The building was insured by the Hartford Fire Insurance Company, which paid a thousand-dollar claim to the county. Commissioners were appointed to plan a new jail and estimate costs. By August the order to fund and construct the existing historic jail was entered into the records. It called for a building "forty feet by twenty feet out to out" with first-story walls three bricks thick, and second-story walls two bricks thick. The pitch (interior elevation) was specified at eleven feet, the "same as the old jail." Plans outlined a central passage eight feet wide in each story, leading to one apartment on either side on each floor, providing a total of four cells. Double doors, one or both with iron bars, would secure the cells. A staircase connecting the upper and lower passage is cited, as are intended twelve- by seventeen-foot dimensions of the cells. The roof was to be "slated on . . . All to be done in workmanlike style." The cost was estimated at about twelve hundred dollars.

Concurrent with this order was a notice placed by Spotsylvania commissioners in the *Virginia Herald* seeking proposals from builders—or undertakers as they were then known. It suggests that the commissioners were busy refining the plans. New ideas, technologies and greater details were contemplated. A spiral stairway was specified, as was lining the lower cells with "bars of iron riveted together cross-wise six or eight inches apart." Sheet iron was mentioned as a covering for the floors. But these were plans, and plans change.

The existing floor plan does not correspond to the historic descriptions cited above. Upon entering the building there is a room, about eight feet wide, running the length of the jail. A wall divides the interior on that long axis, and openings on either side lead to cells. The pattern is repeated on the second level. This layout is alluded to in an 1882 jail report. It is likely, but not certain, that plans changed prior to or during construction.

In March 1855 the jail was nearly complete, and an announcement published in the *Virginia Herald* hinted at the county commissioners' satisfaction in having delivered a top-notch public facility for the administration of justice in the county.

> *The County jail is now nearly completed, and ready for the reception of gentleman boarders! The walls are over two feet in thickness, and the stronger chambers lined with three-inch oak plank. Persons taking quarters will be able to resist all attacks of burglars, and as far as robbers are concerned, may enjoy their slumbers in all the sweetness of a perfect tranquility of mind. It was erected by Mr. Joseph Sanford, as principal contractor, and cost about $3,000.00.*

Though grinning for cameras was not fashionable in the nineteenth century, it does not mean that folks didn't have a sense of humor.

What was Spotsylvania Courthouse like in the 1850s, and what kind of things went on there? This small crossroads hamlet with its spare collection of buildings was certainly a quiet place on most days, with people working in fields, at small industry and at domestic business. But for two or three days each month the regular session of court transformed the county seat into a center of activity and festivity. Court days were an important and much anticipated event in antebellum times, just as they were in the colonial period. While gentleman justices heard cases and attended to administrative business inside the courthouse, citizens outside gathered to discuss and transact business, socialize, canvass, evangelize and seek out amusements.

An anonymous scribe writing for the *Virginia Herald* recorded the events of monthly court in April 1858, enabling a glimpse into the past. Under the heading "Spotsylvania Court-House News," the paper reported a very large attendance, "though we have never seen so little money afloat. The dearth was distressing." Rain was ample that spring, with the Chickahominy River spilling over its banks. Wheat crops were thriving, and most farmers had finished seeding their oat crops.

Candidates for county offices were making the rounds, as were promoters of the *Virginia Baptist*, a new publication about to be launched in Fredericksburg.

Slavery, soon to be condemned by history, was a ubiquitous and ordinary aspect of antebellum life—a condition difficult for the modern mind to comprehend. Deputy Sheriff Mansfield auctioned off the services of some

A view of the intersection where Brock Road meets Courthouse Road, looking northeast. This image is believed to date from the late nineteenth century. The post office and Sheriff Harris's office and home are to the right of Perry's store at the corner in the foreground.

fifteen or twenty bondsmen for the purpose of collecting the delinquent taxes with which their owners were assessed.

Joseph Sanford, the builder of the jail, was again busy with public projects. The *Virginia Herald* reported:

> *Our old friend Sanford has erected large shedding and commodious stabling at the Court House. The yard is on a scale that comports with the energy and enlarged ideas of our worthy court-day host.*

A volunteer rifle company of sixty men was raised, and an exhibition of horses was described as "the best we have ever seen at the Court House. Morgan Hunter, Black Hawk, Orphan Boy, Pamunkey and others attracted much attention by their action and symmetrical proportions."

Joseph F. Walter, "the German," was charged with breaking into a residence and stealing a variety of property. He was tried before an examining court, and scheduled for trial at the next circuit court. The suspect confessed to Officer Timberlake. A stint in jail was forecasted.

The builder of the jail was active, public spirited and had other accomplishments to his credit. After the war he had contracted with the Spotsylvania Ladies Memorial Association to inter 1,035 soldiers at the Confederate Cemetery. The cost of burying the men was about one dollar per interment. The *Virginia Herald* stated in May 1867:

The people gathered at the right are standing by the well where water was taken for the wounded Stonewall Jackson as he was transported via ambulance from Chancellorsville to Guinea Station in May 1836. *Courtesy of Spotsylvania County.*

> *Mr. S. undertook the work as a labor of love, more than one of emolument, as the contract exhibits. Indeed, from his well known liberality, the work would have been done gratis, but for the changed relations that exist in regard to labor.*

A deed book entry indicates that Sanford conveyed the six-acre cemetery site to the "Monumental Association" in March of that year.

Sanford also kept the hotel—then referred to as the Tavern Property—at Spotsylvania Courthouse for many years. Today this building is known as the Spotswood Inn. Its wide portico, an expression of rustic homegrown classicism, anchors the courthouse district with its historic significance. In addition, it enjoys a premier location at the top of the T in the road, where Courthouse Road meets Brock Road. Sanford purchased the Tavern Property—then seated on 1,045 acres—from the estate of Lewis Rawlings in March 1853, one month after the reconstructed Po River Jail burned. The price was $8,901. He sold it in 1869.

He also built the Planter's Hotel in Fredericksburg, which stands today at the northwest corner of William and Charles Streets. Joseph Sanford moved across the river to Stafford after the war, and he died there in 1871.

By 1876 the upper story of the jail was cut off and used for some other purpose. County records indicate that this "impaired the ventilation and health of the jail necessitating confinement of the prisoners in the damp

Two women in the Spotsylvania County Jail. There is a notation on the back of the image in the photographer's hand. It reads in part: "The two girls seen at the door have been there 11 months, have had three trials. They are waiting action of the court on question of law _____ during trial. The charge is assault and larceny." Photo created by J. Brainerd Hall of Worcester, Massachusetts, on May 6, 1887.

cells upon the ground floor." The court ordered the supervisors to restore the upper rooms. Despite the economic collapse and physical devastation characterizing the Reconstruction period, the need for jail space, and by inference the frequency of crime, was low enough to permit the removal of two of the four cells from service.

In February 1913 the jail contained the perpetrator of a tragic and sensational crime, which occurred near McHenry, about two miles from "Brokenbrough," in Spotsylvania County. Nelson Carter, after "quarreling" with his wife Hattie that morning, shot her with a revolver five times after she fled the house. He was arrested by Sheriff Waller and placed in jail at Spotsylvania Courthouse. Hattie was forty years old. According to the *Daily Star*, "They had been living unpleasantly for years."

The case came up before the circuit court on February 28. The defendant entered an insanity plea (homicidal mania), which was supported by expert testimony from doctors traveling from Staunton and Washington, D.C. Crowds at the trial were very large.

In-depth coverage of the trial revealed that Carter had a long-simmering and powerful hatred for his wife. He thought her unfaithful, but several witnesses characterized those notions as unreasonable and unfounded. The prosecution sought a verdict of first degree murder. Testimony revealed that shortly after killing his wife, Carter remarked, "I don't want to be buried within a half-mile of that d— b—. I don't want to be buried near that thing [the dead woman]." He never denied the crime.

The *Daily Star* covered the trial in great detail. A verdict of first degree murder was reached on March 3, and Carter was sentenced to electrocution, scheduled for April 25. The courthouse was "packed to suffocation" as the prosecution asked the jury for protection of society, and a verdict on the law and the evidence. The prosecution stated, "The prisoner had snuffed out the life of one he had sworn to protect." Carter displayed no nervousness as the guilty verdict was read.

The case was appealed to the Supreme Court on the basis of procedural errors, and the sentence was stayed by Governor Mann until June 6. But the court refused a writ of error, and Carter was electrocuted at the state penitentiary in Richmond on June 27, 1913, about four months and three weeks after the murder. He made no final statement. His body, accompanied by his brother and brother-in-law, was put on a train and returned to Spotsylvania County for burial.

On a lighter note, Lewis Dickerson was jailed at Spotsylvania that same year after being indicted for striking Morris Boswell with a bottle and knocking his eye out. He escaped and was later recaptured—he claimed that the jail door had been left open. He later confessed to making a set of duplicate keys, which were recovered and displayed "to a number of interested viewers."

Around 1930 plumbing and electricity were installed in the building, but the jail's serviceable life was, notwithstanding, nearly spent. In 1943 Judge Leon M. Bazile ordered the jail closed on the recommendation and request of the state commissioner of corrections.

> *The County Jail is a fire menace. It is ordered that the jail of the City Of Fredericksburg is designated as the jail for Spotsylvania County so long as the jail remains in its present dangerous condition.*

In 1946 the upper floor of the jail was leased, for one dollar a year, to Rural Telephones of Milford, Virginia. The company installed and operated a telephone exchange there. County officials were eager to facilitate and improve service over a larger portion of the county.

Spotsylvania Preservation Foundation Inc. has recently acquired a lease on the old jail. Preservation plans are in the early stages of development (at

This is a 2007 view of the rehabilitated jail. *Courtesy of the author.*

time of publication in 2008 most of the rehabilitation objectives have been skillfully achieved). Goals include maintenance and conservation measures to further the jail's preservation, and perhaps designing and fabricating for missing building features—especially the iron bars, doors and sashes. Through research, object acquisition, systematic exhibit design and funding, a successful interpretive program can be developed, and the building opened to the public. Benefits would include the attraction of visitors to the courthouse area, the opportunity for education in political, social and architectural history and an improved understanding and appreciation of Spotsylvania's heritage.

Published June 26, 1999.

A Life of Public Service

NINETEENTH-CENTURY SPOTSYLVANIAN SAW MANY CHANGES

Near the close of 1911, Thomas Addison Harris, age sixty-eight, slipped on ice and suffered injuries that confined him to bed at his home at Spotsylvania Courthouse. His health deteriorated, and death claimed him in January 1912. The initial diagnosis was "acute indigestion," according to an obituary in the *Daily Star*.

This unremarkable chain of events (medical diagnosis excepted) is a universally familiar human experience, transcending the limits of culture and time. But T.A. Harris's career did not echo an ordinary script. In the context of local history, his experiences and civic service are noteworthy, and help to illustrate life as it was lived in the Fredericksburg area in another time.

Harris was a Confederate soldier who fought in several principal Civil War battles. During his lifetime, he held four elected posts in the county: superintendent of the poor, commissioner of revenue, sheriff and clerk of the circuit court. He was also, by one account, a successful farmer.

His marriage to Mary Eliza Poole produced two daughters and four sons, one of whom was Dr. William A. Harris, a prominent physician in Spotsylvania County who served three terms in the House of Delegates from 1936 to 1942.

Houses associated with T.A. Harris and his son William remain standing in the courthouse district, adjacent to one another, on the north side of Courthouse Road and opposite the 7-Eleven and the recently closed post office.

The elder Harris was born in Spotsylvania County on August 29, 1844. In May 1861 he rose to defend his native land and enlisted in the Confederate army, Company D, Thirtieth Virginia Infantry. He was seventeen years old.

With the Thirtieth Virginia, he participated in the Seven Days Battles around Richmond in 1862. Though he was entitled to a discharge just

Sheriff Harris can be seen in a photo taken in front of the courthouse. He is the bearded man just left of the central pillar depicted here, wearing a white shirt and hat. His son, William A. Harris, is the child to the left wearing a hat and white clothes. The younger Harris would grow up to be a physician and state lawmaker. *Courtesy of Spotsylvania County.*

prior to his eighteenth birthday, he reenlisted in the Ninth Virginia Cavalry, Company E (Mercer Cavalry of Spotsylvania, first organized in 1859), after spending "some days" back home in Spotsylvania County.

In April 1863 he was promoted to corporal. Shortly thereafter, his regiment fought in the great mounted engagement at Brandy Station in June of that year, and then at Gettysburg where he, according to a "memoriam" published in the *Daily Star* after his death, "by wounds received in battle attested his patriotism and his devotion to his country's welfare."

A biographical sketch, appearing in the *Star* while Harris was clerk of the circuit court, stated that he was with General J.E.B. Stuart "in each of his raids on Pennsylvania and Maryland."

During the battle of Spotsylvania Courthouse in 1864, Harris was present when his regiment screened the Confederate army's right flank and engaged Union troops at Myers Hill. A Civil War Trails interpretive marker installed at Zion Methodist Church notes this fact. Harris partook in the defense of his own backyard and, being native, was detailed as a guide for Stuart's scouts.

The Myers farm lay just east of the church, centered between the Fredericksburg Road (Courthouse Road) and Massaponax Church Road. With its homesite atop a hill, it commanded useful views of Union positions. On May 14, Myers farm was occupied by a small Confederate force, which included the Ninth Virginia and an artillery battery.

Federal troops had resolved to capture that ground, positioning twelve artillery pieces to support the effort. Gordon Rhea, in his book, *The Battles for Spotsylvania Courthouse and the Road to Yellow Tavern, May 7–12, 1864*, writes:

> *These Federal guns soon fired on the Myers house and McGregor's* [Confederate] *Battery responded.*
>
> *When the Southerners spotted the advancing Yankees, they sent a courier with the news to the rest of the troops along the Massaponax Church Road. A member of the 9th Virginia recalled that the brigade bugler sounded "To Horse" and that soon the troopers were galloping forward.*

Superior Union firepower overwhelmed the Confederates, who were "forced to retire, leaving their dead and severely wounded comrades on the field."

Harris served and saw the secessionist cause through to its end. The *Daily Star* article mentioned above also contained this anecdote:

> *At the battle of Five Forks General W.H.F. Lee asked for volunteers to rescue three ladies at the Gilham house, which was between the lines of battle. Mr. Harris was one of the five who volunteered to rescue them, which was done at great risk, both to the ladies and scouts. He received several wounds, and was severely wounded at the battle of Five Forks, a few days before General Lee's surrender.*

After the war, Harris took up (or resumed) the occupation of farmer—an antithetical, and no doubt relieving, change in daily routine, certain to increase his life expectancy. In 1870, his career in local politics and public service began when he was elected superintendent of the poor. This office, formerly called "overseer of the poor," administered relief to the indigent, facilitated the placement of orphans and carried out other responsibilities that affected the social policy of the county government as it was then.

An example of the duties of that office is illustrated in an indenture between Harris (acting on behalf of the court) and Roy A. Jones, a farmer of the county, binding an eleven-year-old orphan named Robert Nelson to an apprenticeship with Jones. It was made in March 1878, the last year of Harris's tenure.

The boy was apprenticed to learn the art of farming. He was expected to live with Jones,

> and remain until he shall attain his full age of twenty-one years, during all of which time, Robert Nelson, his Master shall faithfully serve and obey, his secrets keep, and his lawful commandments willingly do and perform.

In reciprocation, Jones was obligated to, and did, "covenant with the Superintendent and his successor" to instruct the boy in the art of farming in the best manner that he could. Jones was also obligated to provide "sufficient meat, drink, washing, lodging, apparel, and other things necessary for the apprentice."

In contrast with indentures of earlier eras, and underscoring social progress made in the preceding century, Jones was further obligated to teach the boy reading, writing and "common arithmetic as far as the rule of three." He was also required to pay fifty dollars a year, with 6 percent interest, for the apprentice's services. The boy was to receive the money when he reached majority at age twenty-one, and would presumably have had a stake of several hundred dollars with which to start out in life.

Between 1878 and 1883, Harris served as commissioner of revenue for Saint Georges Parish. He ran for sheriff in May 1883, receiving 1,454 votes, trouncing his opponent John W. Carner, who received just 65 votes. Considering Harris's wartime experiences, it is likely that his new job was a better match for the man, affording an occasional opportunity to test his grit.

Shortly after assuming the office of sheriff, in February 1884, Harris one night discovered that the jail's two prisoners had escaped. One had just been convicted of forgery at the January term of court. He was awaiting transport to the penitentiary in Richmond. The other was a petty thief serving four months in the jail.

The night was dark and rainy, and there was nothing to indicate in which direction the prisoners had fled. Wasting no time, Harris enlisted the help of C.J. Chartters and John Payne, the latter reportedly being "well posted about the country through which they wished to travel."

They left the courthouse at about 10:00 p.m., with the fugitives having had about a three-hour head start. The *Virginia Star* reported:

> A little after midnight, by prompt action and quick riding, Mr. Harris was in charge of one bridge, while Messrs. Chartters and Payne held another across the North Anna River, a full twenty miles from the courthouse.

Just minutes after the bridges were reached and posted, Chartters arrested the escaped forger as he was attempting to cross Carr's Bridge and make his way into Louisa County. The other prisoner was not apprehended that night. It was thought that they each took different paths.

The paper reported that the jailbreak was accomplished by cutting through the ceiling

> *some twenty-four feet from the floor* [the front hall portion of the jail's interior, outside of the cells, then had a two-story elevation, undivided by a floor], *passing along the attic, and again cutting through the ceiling over the treasurer's old office, and letting themselves down into that, the door of which quickly gave way to their pressure. Nothing was used by them except a piece of stove-wood and their hands, as the only trouble with them was to reach the ceiling.*

In 1903, Harris was appointed clerk of the circuit court by Judge R.E. Waller, replacing J.P.H. Crismond. Two years later, he was elected to the office without opposition for the full term of eight years, which he never finished.

T.A. Harris farmed land presently occupied by the county office building, the Robert E. Lee Elementary School and the soon-to-be-developed Vakos tract. Harris acquired the parcel, then totaling 259 acres, in 1885 from the estate of Phillip Anns.

A plat created in 1901 indicates that the property line ran along the east side of Brock Road (labeled "The Road to Finchville" on the plat) for nearly three thousand feet, beginning from the rear of the H.F. Chewning Store property, and continuing to a point near Robert E. Lee Drive. The roughly rectangular parcel averaged about sixteen hundred feet in width, with about eleven hundred feet fronting Courthouse Road.

The Folk Victorian house at 9126 Courthouse Road is situated on a parcel that was divided from the farm and presented as a gift by the elder Harris to his son, Dr. William A. Harris, in 1901. The physician built this house shortly thereafter.

The gable front and wing plan was frequently selected by builders between 1870 and 1910, especially in Southern regions. Ornamented porches and jigsaw cut cornice trim, applied to traditional forms, characterize the style. Folk Victorian distinguishes itself from its ostentatious cousins through its comparatively restrained use of ornament, faithfulness to symmetry and absence of multitextured and irregular wall surfaces.

Perhaps the most distinctive feature of this particular building is its curvilinear porch with its roof supported by Ionic columns. The porch design succeeds as an elegant alternative to the usual sawed and turned decoration.

This page and opposite: The folk Victorian house at 9126 Courthouse Road where Dr. William A. Harris once lived still stands. Harris was the son of T.A. Harris who died in 1912 during his tenure as clerk of the circuit court. The house, built in 1901, features a curvilinear porch and Ionic columns. *Courtesy of the author.*

William A. Harris, born in Spotsylvania in 1877, began practicing medicine in the county after his graduation from the Medical College of Virginia in 1900. During World War I, he spent twenty-eight months in the Army Medical Corps and was discharged with the rank of lieutenant colonel. He spent some of that time in France.

As was his father, William Harris was drawn to public office. He served as coroner, health officer and secretary of the board of public roads. He was elected to represent Spotsylvania and Fredericksburg in the House of Delegates in 1935. He served for three consecutive terms, receiving many committee assignments, including roads and internal navigation and moral and social welfare. In May 1944 he died unexpectedly at his home. He was sixty-six years old.

The neighboring house to the east of the one discussed above is also associated with the family. This property was conveyed by the elder Harris to his son Innis in 1899. The building, minus its modern additions, predates William Harris's house and was probably built in the 1880s or 1890s. It cannot be said here whether or not T.A. Harris ever resided there. His known residence and office, at the turn of the century, was located on a

site corresponding to the western end of the county office building parking lot and the now vacated library. That building and others burned down in 1930. Both buildings are presently excluded from the Courthouse Historic District.

T.A. Harris saw a great deal of change in the world, given his life's experience of what is now history. He was a nineteenth-century man, getting from place to place in a buggy and cultivating his land with draft animals. Two mules named Ned and Bet and a horse named John were among the possessions inventoried after his death.

But he was also a founding officer of the Spotsylvania Telephone Co., organized in 1900, and so played an active part in welcoming the future.

Thomas Addison Harris is buried at Zion United Methodist Church in the Spotsylvania Courthouse area along with two other Confederate veterans. Dr. William A. Harris is buried in the Confederate Cemetery at Spotsylvania.

Published October 9, 1999.

It's Good for What Ails Ya

TREE BARK, MADSTONES, TURPENTINE, DIRTY UNDERDRAWERS AND OTHER SOUTHERN FOLK REMEDIES

A young girl in the company of two urchins was peeling back the bark of a wild apple tree in the thick woods near Dunavant, in Spotsylvania County, on the Rapidan River. A man approached and asked the girl what she was doing. The girl replied that her youngest sister was sick with a bad cold, and was coughing all the time. "She keeps a hackin'."

The girl explained:

> The bark of a wild apple tree, if boiled one whole day with a lot of bark, just kept bare covered over with water, will, when given a teacup every time you eats cure any cough or hackin'. But, it will not do any good if the bark is peeled downward. It must be cut into with a knife, and then skinned up, or it will not cure.

It was in the late 1930s when the man, John T. Goolrick of Fredericksburg, recorded this simple event. Goolrick, a former judge, author and journalist, was working for the Virginia Writers' Project (VWP) during the Great Depression. The VWP was the state-sponsored affiliate of the Federal Writers' Project, which was an agency of the Works Progress Administration. Earning twenty dollars a week, VWP field workers recorded the culture and experiences of ordinary folk: life histories, folklore, ex-slave narratives, music and more. American civilization, in its personal and local aspects, was sought, transcribed and archived. Much information was spared from oblivion, which so often has supplanted the historical record of little-noticed people.

The girl in the woods at Dunavant shared another cure:

For a long cold in the head get the leaves of a peach tree, put them in a pot, and boil or steep them until the water turns yellow-dark, and then pour [the water] *off.*

This was used, she said, by putting some in the palm of the hand and "sniffin' it up the nose."

In the backwoods, fields and crossroads-hamlets of the American South the treatment of injury and illness with lay medicine was a persistent tradition, remaining widespread even in the middle of the twentieth century. Reliance on folk and domestic medicine developed and was sustained by simple necessity, and was the historically predominant form of healthcare in sparsely settled areas. People didn't often see doctors for a number of reasons.

Doctors were the elite, and ordinary folk often distrusted them. Besides, access to physicians was spotty and uncertain. For most of the nineteenth century, medical science was frequently based on confused theories, whose implementation in practice often brought disastrous results. People trusted natural medicines, superstition and local wisdom. Professional care was expensive, too. Hard money was generally scarce by today's standards. In addition to a fee for services, doctors would also charge for travel to remote homesteads. The expense and inconvenience of getting a doctor is a powerful and recurrent theme in the history of Southern medicine. Consequently, people practiced lay, folk and domestic medicine.

Folk medicine is the traditional use of homemade remedies learned in a local and informal context. Domestic medicine, which became widespread among the middle class in the second quarter of the nineteenth century, refers to professional knowledge disseminated through books and applied in the home, usually without the assistance of physicians.

Domestic medical manuals provided advice on disease prevention, hygiene, exercise and diet, as well as descriptions of diseases, including symptoms and treatment. Suggestions about when to summon a doctor and how to evaluate their skills and services were included. About a dozen such manuals appeared between 1807 and 1860, with several printed in multiple editions.

But many people, especially those on the geographic and economic margins of society, faithfully practiced traditional cures learned from family and friends, passed along from one generation to the next.

In Dunavant (Rapidan Drive off Ely's Ford Road) Goolrick also collected the medicine of an old black man named Thorton. He told of a "sartin cure" for consumption, or tuberculosis. Balls of gum turpentine, which exudes from and forms on certain kinds of pine trees, were to be chewed and kept in the mouth "constantly."

"This will cure the consumption," the old man said.

A Mr. Ray, "who lived mostly in Spotsylvania County," had a surefire remedy for rheumatism, or neuritis, in drinking a glass of hot milk with a teaspoonful of soda (stir well) three times a day.

As a prescription for snakebite, "several old people" recommended a complicated and unlikely treatment:

> *If a snake bites you, kill a chicken, cut it in half lengthwise before it quits flopping. Remove the entrails and bind the chicken tight about the place where the snake struck, before the chicken gets cold. The poison will all go into the chicken, and the person bitten will then suffer no harm.*

Curative practices among blacks and whites tended to differ, although certain remedies were shared by both groups. Black folks, as indicated by Thorton, set great store in the power of turpentine. When mixed with sugar, it was used to promote the healing of open wounds. The same mixture, ingested in small amounts, would cure stomachaches. In French Louisiana a sore throat was treated by rubbing the neck with a liniment of turpentine, sugar and sulfur. Children with worms were given the juice of smashed "Jimsey" weed with four or five drops of turpentine added.

An expatriate Tennesseean living in New York City was interviewed in 1938 by a member of the Federal Writers' Project. He recalled that blacks back home treating mumps would "rub the oil from three cans of sardines on the cheeks, and then eat the sardines. The swelling would usually go down too. Probably the massaging helped." For headaches they would "take the revenue stamp from a sack of tobacco and paste it on the forehead. It advertised the headache and he would get a lot of sympathy anyway."

Yellow jaundice was treated by placing pure gold against the body. The metal was supposed to draw the disease out of the body and the yellow color out of the skin. An old man suffering from the disease sent his wife to find something of gold to place against his body.

> *She finally managed to borrow a gold wedding ring from a white lady. And they let it lie on the sick man's chest for several days. When he got worse instead of better, the wife toted the ring back to its owner, and reproachfully informed her that "this ring aint no real pure gold—your husban' done give you a just gold-plate ring!"*

Rheumatism was cured by catching a fish and blowing breath into its mouth. "Keep blowing until the fish is dead."

For both black and white folks, a popular cure for warts required "gathering as many pebbles as you had warts, rub one pebble on each wart, take them to a crossroads and throw them over your left shoulder." The warts were supposed to go with them. Another cure for warts was to "take a chunk of dried mud fallen from the hoof of a mule, rub it on the wart. Spit on the underside of the chunk, and then place it on a gatepost."

The informant recalled other fascinating therapies: for a stiff neck, "wrap a pair of underdrawers which have been worn more than two days around the neck."

Stomachache? "Swallow a tablespoon of clean white sand." And for leg cramps, before going to bed, "place patient's shoes against the wall so that the heels do not touch the floor."

As two previous examples of folk healing illustrate, objects—whether animal, vegetable or mineral—were often placed on the body in the belief that contaminants from the afflicted would be drawn out into them. In Virginia during the nineteenth century, the most celebrated and sought-after curative object was the madstone. A madstone was a calculus that occasionally formed in the bladder of deer. A calculus is an abnormal concentration of mineral salts—a stone. Madstones were employed in the treatment of snakebite and the bites of rabid dogs, the latter being an especially pervasive problem then. The threat of being attacked by a mad dog was ever present in an era when foot travel was widespread, and vaccinations and leash laws were unknown in rural areas.

Episodes of dog attacks are recorded with notable frequency in the *Virginia Herald* during the 1800s. In September of 1871 "Mr. James Briggs of Stafford county, who resided near the Old Spotted Tavern, had been badly bitten by a mad dog. The dog was the property of Mr. Briggs, and was highly valued by him." One day, after attacking fowl in the yard, the dog turned on its owner. It seized him by the leg, which fortunately was protected by a stout boot.

The dog then jumped at Briggs' throat, and in warding it off, Briggs was caught and badly bitten on the left arm. Mr. Briggs' son now came up with an axe, by several blows with which the rabid brute was dispatched. No doubt exists that the dog was affected with hydrophobia [rabies].

In September 1876 a mad dog run amok in downtown Fredericksburg created plenty of excitement, and gave several people a terrific opportunity to practice their marksmanship in the heart of the city. The canine attacked a little boy near the Exchange Hotel at Main and Hanover Streets, running

Oral tradition states that this madstone, about an inch and a quarter long, was harvested from a white bull in the nineteenth century and used through the 1930s. *Courtesy of Robert Boutelle, All about Madstones, www.cedarpost.com.*

him into a house unharmed. It then made a "beeline" for another boy. "The dog was at once attacked with pistols, and fired upon, when he made tracks up Hanover Street, and turned into Princes Anne." The report, which would fit so neatly in the *Armed Citizen* section of the National Rifle Association's monthly magazine, continued:

> *Meantime the crowd gathered with their artillery, and the fire was kept up. Two bullets are said to have been shot through the doors of the National Bank, and various bullets lodged in the dog, who kept on making good time.*

The resilient pooch made it to Commerce Street, where

> *he sought refuge in Mr. Kishpaugh's store, but it became too hot for him there* [how this was determined it is not known], *and he left, taking up last refuge in a small house where a colored woman was lying in bed sick.*

There the dog was shot through the head. It took eight bullets before "he succumbed to the necessity of the situation."

In May 1873 a youth named William Martin was bitten by a rabid dog in the vicinity of Central Point in Caroline County. The dog escaped. "Young Martin was taken to Richmond to receive the benefits of the madstone."

A particular madstone was described for a Federal Writers' Project worker in New York interviewing a one-time assistant with a traveling medicine show. The stone belonged to Doc Porter, who headed up "Doc Porters Kickapoo Indian Medicine Show" near the turn of the century.

It was a bluish-gray porous lump about the size of a pullet's egg. It was supposed to cure mad dog or snakebites by sucking the venom out. When pressed against the wound, if it stuck, there was poison in the injury. It would stick until it had sucked itself full of venom, and then fall off. It would then be boiled in milk until it was clean and then re-applied. That was kept up until the madstone wouldn't stick anymore.

One legend had it that madstones were picked up by deer from salt licks, which had fallen from the sky.

The informant recalled seeing Doc Porter use the madstone on a girl who had been bitten on the leg by a copperhead while picking blackberries. "It was in Virginia at a little crossroads place called Smoky Run. It stuck all right. The girl didn't die but she was almight sick."

Madstones with successful histories (those which consistently saved patients from the horror of rabies) became renowned objects in their own right. An effective stone was expensive, amounting to an asset and an investment for the owner. A few in Virginia were known to have exceeded two thousand dollars in price. In 1873 a stone owned by a Mrs. Harrison of Richmond was applied to a little girl who had been bitten by a mad dog in that city.

The stone was applied five times at a cost of $15 per application. The stone had to remain 12 hours each time, and on the final application afforded her great relief; and she is now in good spirits and feeling no pain or inconvenience whatever from the bite.

This particular stone had been applied about three hundred times, with success in every case. It had cost Harrison sixteen hundred dollars, having been bought from Humphrey Sale of Caroline County.

Doctors deriding the effectiveness of madstones were answered with public scorn. A Baltimore doctor questioning the efficacy of madstones in 1871 prompted these remarks in the *Virginia Herald*:

> *The public generally joins in the laugh. There have been too many well authenticated cases of cure for us to accept the opinion of Dr. Smith, learned and prized as he is for high attainments.*

Dr. Bruno Gebhard of the Cleveland Health Museum wrote an essay about folk medicine in 1976 and posited this truth:

> *Folk medicine has one advantage: it has no doubt; it believes. Scientific medicine moves from truth to error to truth—it must search and re-search.*

To people unaccustomed to the movement of truth, the "sartin cure" was sufficient and preferred.

Published March 25, 2000.

Eldorado Fever

EVEN BEFORE THE CALIFORNIA GOLD RUSH OF THE 1850S,
VIRGINIA GOT CAUGHT UP IN THE EXCITEMENT OF
GOLD MINING

In 1829, with Spotsylvania's soil largely wasted from decades of tobacco cultivation and indifference to scientific farming, certain parcels of land were discovered to contain economic potential imagined, but unrealized, by Virginians since the settlement of Jamestown. By June of that year, gold had been discovered on eight plantations in the county. The ensuing forecasts of prosperity aroused hope locally and throughout Virginia. The Old Dominion had been losing stature among the family of American states with its declining standards of living, sloppy agriculture habits, dispiriting rates of emigration and diminishing influence in federal institutions. At that point in time the millennia's imperceptible wearing of the earth had revealed enough of the yellow element to generate some real excitement. In the initial discoveries, rough gold was gathered right off the ground. And in those special locations new pieces of assorted sizes became visible after each heavy rain.

The first publicized discovery occurred on a tract belonging to Captain William F. White and his brother Doctor Edmund White. Their father, John White, gifted the 558 acres to his sons in 1827. The property lay between Robertson Run and Whitehall Creek, just northeast of Shady Grove Corner (Robert E. Lee Drive and Catharpin Road, the latter then called Craigs Road). Gold found at White's and other "mines" in 1829 yielded from undisturbed disintegrated rock (saprolite), or was washed from placer deposits. But such easy pickings would be relatively short-lived. In June 1829 the *Virginia Herald* wrote:

> *Gold of a pure quality is to be found in great quantity in this county. About*
> *$800.00 worth of surface gold (at White's) has been obtained within a*
> *few months, and partial diggings and examinations made in several places*
> *indicates an abundant supply.*

A blue glass bottle shard, a section of pipe and stone walls are among the ruins of Goodwin's Mine, now incorporated into Lake Anna State Park. A large gold mining operation processed ore there in the nineteenth century. The terrain is pockmarked with depressions representing the filled and settled sites of ore shafts. *Courtesy of the author.*

The large Vaucluse gold mine in Orange County was located just north of State Route 3 West, about a mile from the Spotsylvania County line. This mid-nineteenth-century print is captioned "Vaucluse Goldmine, Property of the Orange Grove Mining Company Virginia." *Courtesy of the Library of Virginia.*

The White brothers visited mines in North Carolina (then America's preeminent gold producer) to acquire practical knowledge about techniques. By June 1830 a systematic and highly profitable surface mining operation was underway. The White brothers "were the first to make the discoveries and prove to the world that this section of the country was rich with gold."

Virginia Department of Mineral Resources (VDMR) geologist Palmer C. Sweet described Virginia's gold belt in *Gold in Virginia* (publication 19):

> *The district trends southwesterly from the Potomac River in Fairfax County through Buckingham County and is 12 to 25 miles wide and about 140 miles long. In most cases the gold occurs in sulfide-rich veins and mineralized zones in highly deformed and metamorphosed extrusive and intrusive igneous and sedimentary rocks.*

Locally, gold was also discovered and extracted in the same period, or shortly thereafter, in Stafford, Fauquier, Culpeper, Orange and Louisa.

In 1830 the *Richmond Enquirer*, seeking understanding of the mining process in this region, contacted Mr. John Lewis of Spotsylvania, an educator and a learned gentleman with intimate knowledge of these goings-on (for more about John Lewis see "A Community for Learning"). The resulting

These ruins at Goodwin's mine in southwestern Spotsylvania may have supported a sluice. The source of water for this mine was Pigeon Run, which today composes the eastern boundary of Lake Anna State Park. *Courtesy of the author.*

written response from Lewis described conditions and illustrated how it was done. His florid, spare-no-detail prose appeared in the *Virginia Herald*. His correspondence has been pruned and paraphrased here for economy.

> *Gold appearing in pieces from specks to forty pennyweight (two ounces) was sufficiently abundant in proportion to other matter to justify separation.*

It was found on the surface and to depths of four feet in strata of disintegrated and irregular quartz, on high ground and along streams and rivulets where the richest deposits were found in blue clay resting upon decomposed slate. The nascent mining process was virtually identical at all sites at this time.

> *The earth was dug up and carried to the nearest stream, and thrown on a sieve of wire, or perforated wheel iron, placed on one end of a semi-cylindrical trough, like a canoe.*

This device—the washer (also referred to as a rocker)—was mounted on pivots at the end, and was rocked like a cradle as water was poured over earth placed in the sieve. Material light enough to "swim" was carried off.

Heavier substances, the larger caught by the sieve, were taken up. Gold grains and particles passing through the sieve subsided at the bottom, where quicksilver was introduced to form an amalgam. The amalgam was prevented from exiting the far end with water and waste by a series of transverse ledges (riffles) fastened to the bottom of the washer. Gold caught by the mercury was separated by heat concentrated with blow pipes, and the quicksilver would recondense and be reused. "About three fourths of the gold obtained is in the amalgam."

Lewis's "canoe" was essentially a sluice box, though he did not use that term. The rocking feature added an interesting dimension and may have represented technology developed here, or perhaps imported from the gold fields of North Carolina.

Lewis also described operating expenses and provided a representative return on investment, citing Johnson's mine.

> Labor employed, expenses incurred, etc., at these surface mines are nearly alike, and may be approximate from one datum—the number of washers employed. I am acquainted with the details at Johnson's and will give them.

Fixtures, Dams, Log Houses, Cart Horse, Tools.	$500.00
Labourers, three men, two boys, one woman	$468.00
superintendant, food.	$968.00

> From Aug. 1829, to Aug. 1830, from this investiture and expense, the result has been, in Gold found within the same time,

and sold in New York and Philadelphia.	$3,845.39
Sent on to be sold, worth certainly.	$2,660.00
Returns-total value.	$6,505.39

It is reasonable to assume that the labor referred to above was mostly bonded—in other words, slave.

The rudimentary process described was only effective for working surface deposits. The exploitation of these depleted accessible bullion and led to the discovery of underground veins. At the time Lewis was writing, exploratory shafts were sinking in Orange. Virginia's hard-rock (lode) gold mining industry was born—its quickening first detected here.

What Lewis referred to as "Eldorado Fever" and "Mexican Measles" swept over the region. Zealous, misdirected and disorganized treasure seekers squandered time and money, meeting disappointment. "Gold Land for Sale" notices frequently appeared in newspapers. Farmers curtailed their regular labors, panned for gold and leased land with the intention of substituting gold-related revenue for traditional income generated from cash crops. In the year Lewis's description was written, there were five serious mining operations in Spotsylvania: Johnson's, White's, Taylor's, Richard's (of New York) and Goodwin's.

There was concern about slackening interest and energy devoted to cultivation and husbandry, and contemplative people viewed events with some ambivalence and trepidation. Arcadian society, idealized in allegorical paintings of picturesque rural life in harmony with neighbors and God's creation, was widely embraced in Virginia and across America at that time. Though the realities of life in Spotsylvania County in the 1830s were probably, for most folks at least, more brutish than idyllic, a way of life (agriculture—Jefferson's matrix of liberty and Republican virtue) was perceived to be threatened. The following editorial comment appearing in an 1831 issue of the *Virginia Herald* epitomizes this concern.

> *What changes are to be effected in our national character and condition, should these developments continue as they have commenced, is a question of no little interest. While we would not reject the golden treasure we are free to confess our belief that in the patriarchal simplicity of our fathers, and the peaceful pursuits of agricultural life, will always be found our greatest degree of prosperity and happiness-and surely no quality or profession accords so well with the genius of our institutions.*

An environmental alarm was also sounded. Writing in 1830 as witness to an extensive, highly profitable operation in Pittsylvania County, a newsman offered this thought:

> *We cannot but believe that gold mines are highly injurious to any country in which they exist. Such at least has been the experience of other counties.*

It didn't take long for Virginia's gold mining industry to pass into its corporate phase. Exploitation of underground veins, or lode deposits, required a higher level of organization, scientific knowledge, skill and capital. The new process was summed up neatly by William H. Gaines Jr., in the article "Piedmont Bonanza," appearing in the *Virginia Cavalcade*.

> *That process required the sinking of shafts deep into the ground, the digging of cross-tunnels, called adits, along the veins, and the installation of machinery to pump passages clear of water, to raise the ore to the surface*

and crush and grind it. In some veins the surrounding rocks were so hard that blasting by gunpowder was necessary.

Gold mining now required substantial capital investment in heavy equipment: steam engines for pumping water, raising and grinding ore and sawing timber; stamping machines for reducing ore, with accompanying head stamps, troughs, plates and lifting cams; amalgamating mills with iron gearing; cast-iron pumps and pipe by the hundreds of feet, with screw bolts and joints; laboratory equipment for analysis and finishing work; and a long list of other tools and implements. Labor and material was also invested in the building of numerous structures as the mines took the form of work-camp communities.

Enter the "Northern Capitalists." The Virginia Mining Company of New York was the first to incorporate, receiving its charter from the General Assembly in 1832, two years before the *Virginia Herald* reported:

> *Messrs. Whites of this county have lately sold their gold mines to a mercantile house in New York for the comparatively small sum of thirty-thousand dollars.*

For a time the company also operated the Vaucluse Mine in Orange County, as well as other sites along the Rapidan. Whites' mine became known as Whitehall, for which the creek near Shady Grove Corner was named. Throughout the antebellum period, after the war and for much of the remainder of the nineteenth century, Northern interests factored heavily in gold mining operations here.

Entrepreneurial vision, engineering expertise and capital drifted down from Baltimore, Philadelphia and New York. Between 1832 and 1837 sixty-five companies were chartered by the General Assembly.

In 1834 the freshly minted United States Mining Company announced its intention to sell its stock in either Philadelphia or New York. The United States mine was located just south of the confluence of the Rapidan and the Rappahannock Rivers, and east of where Hunting Run spills into the Rapidan. "It is believed that all shares will be bought there (up north)," stated the *Virginia Herald*.

> *But local citizens will be afforded the opportunity to subscribe. Books of subscription will be opened at the store of Messrs. Wm. Jackson Junior and son. Those wishing to see specimens of ore, call at said store.*

This page and opposite: The mill house chimney of the Vaucluse mine survives. Basement and foundation ruins lie adjacent to the chimney. *Courtesy of the author.*

This image of the Belzoro gold mine in Goochland County appeared in *Harper's Weekly* in 1865. This depicts a simple surface mining and sluicing operation. It is the kind of mine that would have existed in Spotsylvania in the 1830s. *Courtesy of the Library of Virginia.*

William Jackson Jr. operated one of the leading dry goods stores in Fredericksburg, having learned the business under his father while the family was living for a time in New York. He was president of United States Mining Company. He also acquired and mined a homestead tract called Greenwood, northwest of Chancelorsville. Jackson was said to have been "seized with the gold fever." Excessive groundwater put a crimp in the Greenwood operation, and United States Mining, under Jackson, was declared unprofitable and was abandoned by 1837. After gold was discovered in California in 1849 Jackson, in collaboration with a party from Richmond, bought and freighted a ship and sailed for that land of promise. So did many other Virginians with experience in the gold fields. Jackson had engineering talent and is credited with improving the rockers used to wash out gold. Many of those devices were brought out to California with him, perhaps influencing technology used there.

The Virginia Mining Company got into trouble with its stock offering in the closing months of 1833. Its agents were accused of circulating fraudulent information about the quality of tested ore retrieved from operations just getting underway in Spotsylvania and Orange. Corporate officers had sent ore to be tested in New York by "men of celebrity as assayers." The resulting analysis and report "raised in the public mind the most extravagant hopes of success—success beyond all precedent in mining annals."

Consequently applications for stock far outpaced available shares. To its credit, the Virginia Mining Company refrained from selling additional shares until the mines could yield a steady profit. With the company refusing to sell and investors holding tight, outstanding shares were bid up furiously. Virginia Mining was initially offered at one hundred dollars per share. Human nature shot it up to five hundred dollars. Some people got burned.

What happened? It was later reported that the assay process was flawed. The assays were made in the crucibles by fluxing the ore with alkali and lead,

> *a process to obtain every atom of gold in the ore. Whereas amalgamation, the process used on the large scale, can only take up that portion of gold which is free from the encrusting of the sulphurate and oxides of iron.*

In other words, the assay was factoring in gold that would never be retrieved from the ore with the industrial-scale production technology then available. The company's honor was upheld, but legislators in Richmond henceforth devoted increased scrutiny to applications of incorporation submitted by gold mining interests.

How much gold was produced in Virginia? State Department of Mineral Resource tables provide the source for these historical peaks and valleys. Production figures for 1829–1879 are from the U.S. Bureau of Mines. The value of gold stood at about twenty dollars per ounce throughout most of this nation's history. In the year of the Whites' discovery, 121 Troy ounces were reported. By 1833, 5,031 ounces were taken. The years 1834, 1835 and 1836 each resulted in about 3,000 ounces. The year in which the most gold was produced ironically coincided with the discoveries at Sutter's Mill in California. In 1849, 6,259 ounces were produced. By 1857, production had plummeted to 195 ounces. Except for 1860, which saw 1,045 ounces reported, production in Troy ounces would be measured in three digits until 1937. The Civil War years 1861 to 1865 saw 536, 15, 3, 0 and 44 ounces respectively. Following that, the nineteenth century's best year was 1882, with 726 ounces.

As the figures indicate, the War Between the States had a distracting influence on gold mining. But by 1867 there was "quiet activity pervading the mining interests in this section of Virginia," according to the *Virginia Herald*, promising yields "far different from the flash era, when gold mines were 'salted,' and held generally as objects of speculation." By November of that year, seventeen mines in Spotsylvania, Culpeper, Orange and Louisa were expected to be in full operation.

A New York concern running Smith's mine, located on a bend in the Rappahannok near Pipe Dam Run, had sunk a fifty-five-foot shaft. About forty tons of ore were waiting for crushers to become operational.

A Philadelphia company had just purchased five hundred acres containing the Mitchell mine, near Whitehall, for sixteen thousand dollars. Gold production reported during Reconstruction was in the mid-hundreds of ounces statewide.

If Smith's mine can serve as an indication, carpetbagger mining interests didn't fare too well. One hundred acres of Smith's tract were sold in trust for fourteen hundred dollars one year after its purchase. The sale of mining machinery fetched another nine hundred dollars.

In a scene that likely played out several times over the decades, robbery and subsequent shooting occurred at Goodwin's mine in April 1870. Goodwin's was located on Pigeon Run south of Route 601 in Spotsylvania. One particular day a vein of "solid gold" had been uncovered. The *Fredericksburg Ledger* reported that it only took a few minutes to take out several hundred dollars.

> *On leaving the property for the night they left a guard of three men with loaded guns, to protect the gold that was still in sight. About nine o'clock the next morning, a Sunday, two workmen from the mine were discovered to have sneaked in, and were caught collecting gold from the vein. They were ordered immediately out by the guard who had come suddenly upon them, and not going soon enough, one of the guards fired upon them three times.*

The men, obviously afflicted with the gold fever, escaped without injury. Warrants were sworn out for their apprehension.

Another drama—a tragedy in two acts—that found its way into the papers concerned an unlucky Mr. James McPherson, who was the manager of the Rappahannok Gold Mine in Stafford. He lost his home, furniture and apparel to fire in 1887. An adjoining commissary building also burned down. McPherson was taken in by a good citizen of Fredericksburg until he could rebuild. The year before, McPherson barely escaped death while working at the mine:

> *He was endeavoring to reverse the belt on the machinery that operates the stamp mill, and was caught in the belting and carried to the shafting with such force as to break an arm, and was otherwise painfully bruised.*

As gold can be searched for and not found, it can also be found while not searching for it. In 1890 the *Free Lance* informed its readers that a man sinking a well in northern Spotsylvania struck "an immense vein" at a depth of about twenty-five feet. "He got a lump of gold worth several hundred dollars." Experienced miners were called and pronounced it a rich and promising vein.

Little remains on the surface today to testify to this important, frenzied industry, whose mercurial history is aptly symbolized by the essential gold-catching quicksilver itself. Gold fever produced thirty-nine mines and prospects (field checked by VDMR) in Spotsylvania alone. Today there are only two permitted gold mines in the entire state of Virginia, according to VDMR geologist Palmer Sweet. One is in Goochland (Southern Piedmont Mining), and the other in Pittsylvania (Gold Crown Mining).

Buildings that supported the historic mines were probably utilitarian and ephemeral. Scavengers and natural forces, in partnership with time, have eaten them up. What remains mostly are stone foundations (with protruding bolts ready to trip the unwary), rusting scraps of light-gauge metal, occasional shards of glass and the pits and trenches that gave ore to the ponderous stamping mills.

Amid the overgrown ruins of an isolated gold mine, sounds from the past may be summoned through imagination: shouts of men, whirring belts, hissing, belching steam boilers, iron or steel pulverizing ore, the discordant friction and collision of mechanical apparatus in motion, draft animals straining before creaking, loaded carts, shovels scratching gravel, the gut-vibrating shock of an explosive charge.

It is long gone, replaced with burbling creeks, the sounds of birds and squirrels at play and work and the muffled, modulating hum of tires on asphalt.

It has been a long time since the fever subsided.

Published April 29, 2000.

Whole Lotta Sheds Goin' On

OUTBUILDING COLLECTION ILLUSTRATES A PAST LIFESTYLE AND A DIMINISHING VIRTUE

I like to drive country roads. I enjoy the things I can see through my windshield: things like thriving corn rows, cool dark stands of pine, brilliant carpets of grain, lush pastures, ditch blossoms and all the colorful prosperity of creation.

I can spot wildlife like bounding white-tailed deer; ubiquitous turkey vultures, those homely hang gliders ascending effortlessly on currents of heated air; scurrying vigilant groundhogs; black-eyed rabbits and more. I enjoy the loitering bovines, simple-minded and carefree and just bright enough to cluster in shaded muddy pools on burning days.

Best of all are the man-made landscape features, the cultural texture of the land serving as the fingerprints of a place, proving its distinct identity. I am thinking of things like homemade mailboxes, ambitious collections of lawn ornaments and old houses nestled among magnificent, aged shade trees, carefully arranged sapling-dreams of some departed soul anticipating the coolness and joy they would someday bring, if only for the next generation.

Old barns and outbuildings wear the inimitable patina of time, signaling what was useful and important to daily work in bygone times. Independent country stores offer relief from the formulaic convenience store arrangement and its tiresome saturation. What the little stores lack in inventory is offset by their human authenticity and independence.

I had been curious about an especially large collection of old sheds and outbuildings sitting on a small farm in Brokenburg, on State Route 208—a veritable "shedopolis," if you will. No two are alike in shape, size or detail. Building materials are mostly the flotsam and jetsam of the prewar Piedmont: corrugated and sheet metal, rough-sawed planks and lumber, composition roofing and siding shingles, old sashes, posts, castoff fixtures and hardware and the like.

These are a few of the sheds dotting the landscape on the late Percy Sacra's Spotsylvania County property. Dating to the 1930s and '40s, the small utilitarian structures are a testament to Sacra's dedication to thrift. *Courtesy of the author.*

This shed is clad with discarded printing plates from the *Free Lance-Star* newspaper. Images and text were visible for some time after their installation. *Courtesy of the author.*

I was attracted to this visual cacophony and to its uniqueness and its rebellious disregard for mainstream aesthetics—namely harmony, cohesion and fastidiousness. The whole arrangement is quaint, clustered and cozy, forming a nice roadside composition.

One day I stopped at the place, knocked on the door and prepared to pose a nosy question. A woman came to the door. I introduced myself.

"Can you tell me about these sheds? They look kind of interesting and there are so many of them."

Dora Dobson, the lady of the house, was nice to this curious stranger. She lives there with her momma, Sue Sacra. "Well there ain't much to tell," she said.

And maybe that's true. But there is a little more to tell about the nature of daily labor for people in Spotsylvania County years ago and what used to be important.

Percy Sacra of Spotsylvania never wasted a thing. That's why it all looks the way it does. The late Mr. Sacra bought the place in the 1920s from "an old man," I was told. There was a two-room shack and he added to it. His wife of fifty-four years, Sue, still lives there. She has never lived more than a couple of miles from that place.

The Sacras lived their prime during the Depression. He farmed and worked at Pulliam's sawmill, which was across the road from their house.

Percy Sacra working his fields with a Farmall tractor. The house in the background is extant. *Courtesy of Dora Dobson.*

She tended to home and farm. Percy Sacra was fortunate enough to get a job at the FMC Cellophane Plant. He never went back to sawmill work, where the repeated turning of logs being sawed left a "knot" on his hip. Factory work paid better. FMC operated a bus to bring rural workers to the factory.

The FMC plant was a godsend for the area in the 1930s, when crop prices were severely depressed. In 1933, about one-quarter of Spotsylvania farmland was hammered away by auctioneers. In May 1935, the *Free Lance-Star*'s front page declared that Fredericksburg was the only place in Virginia "where the number of persons employed and the amount of wages increased simultaneously," according to the 1933 biennial census of manufacturers.

Percy Sacra's dedication to thrift is preserved and illustrated in those eighteen sheds, barns and outbuildings he erected on his farm. Most were put up in the 1930s and 1940s. They were designed and laid out by their maker, shaped by his experiences and needs.

Dobson, Sacra's daughter, described her father as tidy and organized in his work. He apparently enjoyed building and banging nails. He expanded his workshop twice, so that the elongated outbuilding was built in three phases, using different roofing and cladding materials in each phase, of course.

Dobson assured me, "Daddy really believed in nails. When he put something out, it wasn't gonna fall down no time soon."

Percy Sacra in Spotsylvania with his Model A Ford. *Courtesy of Dora Dobson.*

True. Selection of material was driven by availability and habits were born from experience, which disallowed useful things to be wasted. The buildings are a tribute to resourcefulness.

Thrift is defined as wise management of money and resources. It is a virtue like charity and honesty demonstrating, in part, gratitude for having possessions. Whether by intention or consequence, it shows respect for the industry of neighbors known and unknown, and for natural resources.

Evidently, Sacra was a big-time recycler, likely accomplishing more than most present-day environmental activists ever could. Luckily, his consciousness was spared banal phrases like "save the planet."

I suspect thrift is widely considered old-fashioned and obsolete in our consumption-crazed society, like doilies carefully arranged over the back cushions of a mohair sofa. But thrift is not on the verge of extinction. It is just not nearly as widespread as it once was. When Sacra needed material for a fence, he found it at the dump. Once, he collected old mattress springs and used them as fence sections fastened to posts driven into the ground. This kind of a fence was an embarrassment to his daughter at the time, but was surely effective and cheap. I wouldn't bet on any chicken breeching a bedspring fence.

An inventory of the buildings by use sheds light on a kind of life that has, for the most part, disappeared. The last and largest building Sacra put up was the barn. There's a chophouse where cow chop and horse chop (silage) were milled for those animals. A henhouse stands adjacent to that, then a tractor shed and a workshop. A very long equipment shed sits way out back, screening a couple of vestigial privies.

There's a pigpen, a smokehouse and a summer kitchen. I believe the summer kitchen was used mostly for eating, to escape the heat in the house generated by cooking and flies drawn by food preparation.

"We had no screens, and flies was plentiful," Sue Sacra recalled.

As food was prepared and set out, someone would be assigned a leafy branch to wave over the table to shoo them away.

A children's playhouse was identified, though with all the little structures, I imagine there was no shortage of snug secret places for kids, reasonably safe from the intrusion of grown-ups and conducive to the exercise of dreams.

The mill house stands right across the highway, opposite the house. It used to shelter a steam engine that Sacra used to grind grain into meal. The engine burned wood.

Finally, a half-dozen various sheds, not counting expansions, dot the property. Together, they compose the infrastructure of a small farm of that era, hammered together during hard times, making some measure of prosperity possible. These utilitarian buildings are a reminder of a more

Privies still stand where they were built. *Courtesy of the author.*

A surviving section of bedspring fence. *Courtesy of the author.*

Percy Sacra's widow, Sue Sacra, *right*, sits with her daughter Dora Dobson on a glider at the Sacra home. Sue Sacra recalls a time when farms were self sufficient and "there wasn't much occasion to go to Fredericksburg." *Courtesy of the author.*

self-sufficient lifestyle that was common before Spotsylvania became heavily suburbanized, when many people were still fused with the land.

Sacra raised hogs, cows and chickens and grew corn and wheat as farmers in Spotsylvania had done for generations. A kitchen garden and some fruit trees could round out a family diet.

"There wasn't much occasion to go to Fredericksburg," recalled Sue Sacra. "People didn't have to go. We went maybe twice a year, for a doctor or something. Sugar, matches, coffee and soda were all that you needed."

Those items could be picked up at country stores, such as Luck's Store and Carr's Store in Brokenburg. Men wore bib overalls day in and day out. Women wore long cotton dresses with long sleeves that they made themselves. Traditional notions of modesty were slow to wither out in the county.

Big events included hog-killing days and wheat-"thrashing" times. Those were big cooking days. Dora Dobson remembers, "Daddy would make straw stacks and that was the plaything. The kids would swim in the wheat."

With conviction, Sue Sacra summed up her recollections, framing a paradox perhaps as old as human thought itself. "People lived then poor and hard-up. We were more happy then. People have too much right now."

Published September 2, 2000.

A Community for Learning

SPOTSYLVANIA'S LLANGOLLEN SCHOOL FOR BOYS
FLOURISHED IN THE NINETEENTH CENTURY AS A
BACKWOODS ACADEMIC VILLAGE

A University should not be a house but a village," wrote Thomas Jefferson. The founder of the University of Virginia believed that collective life was essential to an optimal educative environment.

Educator John Lewis of Spotsylvania, Jefferson's contemporary, once penned his intention to "form a little community, in a healthy and retired situation, where a small number of pupils might find all that is necessary for the development and cultivation of the body and the mind." He did that in November 1814 when he opened the Llangollen School for Boys, the first important and professionally administered school to operate in the county of Spotsylvania. Evidence gives every indication that Lewis was a passionate and dedicated educator. He earned a reputation as a scholar and a man of letters among his contemporaries. With uncommon stamina, carefully reasoned convictions and a searching intellect, he painstakingly molded Llangollen into a respected and essential institution, providing intellectual and moral training to the youth of this area's leading families.

The Llangollen School community was situated on a 345-acre plantation of the same name, near the North Anna River in the southern part of the county. It was split off from an adjacent plantation called Belle Air, owned by his father Zachary Lewis. The name *Llangollen* recalls the ancestral home of the Lewis family in Wales. Contemporary accounts describe it as a "neighborhood" consisting of several buildings—a backwoods, vernacular academic village, idyllic and healthful, blessed with an abundance of good food, water and air. "The surrounding country is distinguished for its salubrity," wrote Lewis, in a letter to the *Richmond Inquirer* in 1826. "The spot where the school is located has been remarkably beautiful, no death having occurred among pupils, teachers or children." He noted that since "the commencement of the institution" the average number of students residing at Llangollen was thirty-three per year.

John Lewis was born into the prosperous planter class in 1784. He was educated and groomed for the law as his grandfather, father and uncles before him. Lewis was well positioned for that successful career, but his desire to teach was dominant and distracting. Realizing that he needed to broaden his knowledge if he was to fulfill his dream of establishing and operating a successful school, he secured a tutor, the Reverend Hugh Boggs, rector of Berkley Parish. He also immersed himself in independent study, readying himself to teach, while simultaneously designing educational theories.

In 1811 he gave up law and advertised his intention to open a school at Belle Air. This was Lewis's first school and it was not yet known as Llangollen. His plan was to enroll about fifteen students ages nine to fifteen. Instruction consisted of reading, grammar, geography, composition, criticism, history, Latin and "the inferior branches of mathematics."

When the War of 1812 began, Lewis was already enlisted in the Spotsylvania Troop of Cavalry, belonging to the Second Regiment, Second Division of the Virginia militia. His initial enlistment was certified in 1807 when he was commissioned a second lieutenant.

He attained the rank of captain and led the Spotsylvania Cavalry in patrolling the shores of the Potomac.

While Lewis was serving in the militia, the school at Belle Air was being managed by his wife, the Reverend Boggs and John Lawrence, an assistant teacher probably plucked from the roster of students at Belle Air. While on duty in the field Lewis came down with "camp fever." Plans he was developing for the new and enlarged school were briefly postponed.

By 1813 the Llangollen School and the main dwelling house were taking shape. An account book entry dated May 1813 lists disbursements for sawing and dressing plank and timber, a lathe, sundry hardware (including cut nails, hinges and screws), hauled shells (lime), glass and bonded labor. Spotswood Crenshaw received about four hundred dollars for building. Shortly thereafter, in very large letters written with flourish, he recorded the birth of his dream atop a page in his account book: "John Lewis removed from Belle Air to Llangollen on the 24th of November, Anno Domini, 1814."

Then, as now, the cost of education could only go up. Annual tuition at Belle Air was $75, including board, washing, candles and fire. When the school was moved and remade as Llangollen the cost rose to $140. Bedding and bedclothes were extra. The new school was an expanded and refined version of the one conducted at Belle Air. Capacity for enrollment was doubled and the curriculum and administrative philosophy showed signs of expansion and maturation.

John Lewis's house survives as one of Spotsylvania's important historic buildings. It was turned out in the vernacular Federal style. The house

Headmaster John Lewis's house is all that survives of the 345-acre Llangollen academic community, which began operating in 1814. *Courtesy of the author.*

anchored the academic community and the plantation, serving as Lewis's dwelling and as an administrative and reception center for the school. There are two front doors, one opening into a "reception hall" once used to receive patrons and guardians of pupils. This room contains an elaborate fireplace surround with Ionic columns flanking the hearth. It is the largest room in the house.

Lewis's children were housed upstairs beneath the steeply pitched gable roof where two separate two-room apartments are accessed by their own staircases. The stairs leading to the daughters' rooms are adjacent to the downstairs rear bedroom where Lewis and his wife slept. A staircase accessed from the west parlor, in the front of the house, led to the sons' chambers.

The building's rectangular chimneys are noteworthy, being set way inward from the gable ends, like those of fine eighteenth-century English Georgian houses. Ordinarily a house of this form would have end chimneys. The orientation of these chimneys is distinctive because the wide dimension is parallel to the ridge, viewed facing the eaves.

There was once an addition on the westerly side of the house. It sat atop a basement entered through a "cellar-hut." It was used as a dining hall. The addition also housed a nursery on the main level and a dormitory in the garret for the youngest boarding pupils. Though the addition was dismantled long ago, an indentation can be seen on the ground outlining its footprint, likely because fill has settled into the basement.

No one living today knows precisely what the Llangollen School community looked like. Word-of-mouth descriptions and accounts handed down across generations have been recorded, providing scarce insight into the physical nature of the place.

One writer, Howard Meriweather Lovett, described the Lewis home as being "without architectural grace. The charm was in the setting, in a vale bounded by wooded hills." There was a terraced garden in the back that led to a creek and a pond where boys skated in winter and swam in summer. On all sides of the house were fruit and flowers. "I planted purple *lilacks* in the front and rear of the house, and ten Morello cherry trees above the spring," wrote Lewis in 1814. He also set out roses, hyacinths, violets, chrysanthemums, narcissus, snowballs and all sorts of edible berry bushes.

A spring—which was so abundant that a well was never needed in Lewis's time—lay west of the house. Near the creek below the garden the headmaster had built himself a one-room office with a large fireplace. In it was a bath used by the men and boys in the community. "A trap door in the floor opened into a pool which was filled by pipes bringing water from the branch, making a primitive kind of sunken bath."

In front of the Lewis house was a driveway leading to the public road.

> *On each side of this driveway were rows of excellently constructed hewn log cabins with fireplaces, picturesque and comfortable lodgings for the young gentlemen who attended the school. The school itself was a larger cabin built in 1815.*

It contained a loft that was used as a dormitory.

> *These smoothly hewn log cabins were dovetailed at the corners with skill. The cracks between the logs were striped and the inside walls white washed, making a dwelling that was warm in winter and cool in summer, as comfortable as the brick dwellings from which many of the pupils came to Llangollen.*

Pauline Poindexter, a descendant of Dr. Richmond Lewis, elder brother of John, was living at Belle Air in the 1890s. Mrs. Poindexter wrote about Llangollen in 1950, recalling her first visit to the place.

> *We were shown the cabins for the young men, that is, where they had been located, ranged around the edge of the yard to the front and along*

the driveway leading out. We were told how a path led through the Belle Air woods, and midway was the "Sunset Tree," also called the "Trysting Tree," where young people, boys and girls did meet, and had many social and school gatherings.

Some of the boy's names were written on the once white basement walls where they were still to be seen. I can't imagine the headmaster John Lewis allowing the scribbling of names on his walls—but they were there—put there no doubt in after years by a party of former students returned to these deserted halls.

John Holladay, a pupil of John Lewis's who went on to serve in the House of Delegates, kept a commonplace book while attending Llangollen in 1824. It is filled almost entirely with verse. The final page contains a fable in the style of Aesop, and most interestingly, admonishments in the headmaster's bold and heavy hand: "Immodest words, Beware John Holladay." Farther up the page he noted "Inattention," with signature and date attached. At the bottom of the page Holladay, no doubt compelled by teacher Lewis, wrote this cautionary sentence twenty-six times: "Command you may, your mind from play, every hour in the day."

Lewis's views on education were comprehensive and carefully crafted. Most aspects of the Llangollen system were grounded in truths that will survive in perpetuity. His outlook was in some ways progressive. His standards were high lest pupils be shortchanged.

Art and beauty deserved devotion, and begged pursuit.

We deem it to be among the most important and interesting duties of a teacher, to place before his pupils frequently in their most lovely and attractive forms, all the virtues which constitute the ornament and dignity of man, and which build up his utility and happiness on the sure and steadfast foundation of love, obedience and gratitude to God, the giver of all good.

Corporal punishment was believed to be futile as correction and contrary to man's better nature.

Punishment can only force or restrain, and are not productive of the desire of virtue or knowledge. We cannot punish into anyone the love of virtue, and without this exists in the heart, there is no valuable or vital principal of moral excellence.

It was only to be used as a last resort.

Lewis recognized the importance of physical education and moral and civic training. He carefully considered student nutrition and closely supervised matters of diet.

> *Health requires in young persons, not only the judicious use of nutritious substances, but great caution in regards to stimulants. Boys whose growth is not complete require more food than men. It should be abundant and nutritious. But simply and plainly prepared, not various at the same meal, but frequently varied at different meals. Sleep should be at regular intervals and guarded from unnecessary or alarming interruptions.*

Llangollen was largely self-supporting when it came to provisions. Standard imports—sugar, coffee, tea, chocolate and rice—were purchased. All else was grown, raised and processed on the farm, or bartered from neighbors. The variety and quantities of food noted and discussed in Lewis's account books is remarkable. Records mention "meats for every day: ham (middling, shoulder, jowl), fish, chicken, ducks, turkey, beef; vegetables and hot breads made from home-grown water-ground flour and meal."

The fall hog butchering coinciding with the year of Llangollen's opening yielded five thousand pounds of pork. A large variety of fruits are noted in Lewis's copious agricultural notes.

Vegetable seeds were sown as early as February sometimes, after the gardens were prepared. On February 10, 1819, Lewis wrote:

> *Manured my garden and worked the borders. Fifty good horse-cart-loads of well rotted manure annually will do a garden of one acre.*

Llangollen incorporated military training into its system. Lewis believed that there was great value in exercises, drills and military instruction. "They tend to give an erect and easy carriage, healthy as well as graceful, and may be necessary in the defense of our country and homes." He believed that an instinct for obedience and order, and a capacity for concentrated action, complemented and enhanced scholastic discipline and achievement.

> *The object should be to lead the mind to the love of virtue and the desire for knowledge, as the means of doing good. We have, therefore, military training. Physical education is thus made to cooperate with moral and intellectual culture. The union of these, we believe, constitutes the best system of instruction. There is no good system in which they are not united.*

Winter and summer uniforms for boys were described:

For winter—a black gray coat with standing cape, yellow metal buttons and a black star on each side of the cape; pantaloons of the same cloth with the coat; dark waistcoat with yellow metal buttons; and a round black hat on parade. For summer: a blue coat with standing collar and a white star on each side of the cape. Pantaloons of light grayish white material; waistcoat white. White metal buttons to the whole summer suit.

Lewis employed the inductive method of instruction, reasoning from the particular to the general. This was especially true for teaching modern languages derived from Latin. "The order of the study is arranged, that what has been acquired is made the instrument of acquiring more."

He believed then, as most do today, that it is healthy and right that young people's time be adequately filled with scholastic, creative and athletic activities. "Of morals and discipline we trust much to the constant active occupation of the body and mind."

As a scholar Lewis's principal strengths lay in languages and letters. In 1819 he was advertising in the *Virginia Herald*, referring to Llangollen as a "Grammar School intended to prepare boys for college or university." He was a familiar contributor to Virginia newspapers, writing on varied subjects from protective tariffs to gold mining. He was an aesthetic and had a strong interest in poetry. Late in his life Lewis compiled and edited a book of verse, *Flowers and Weeds of the Old Dominion*, published in 1859. The poet-compiler realized that some of the collected verse was not excellent in quality—these were the weeds. He wrote:

But weeds to the philosophic mind, are productions indicating conditions of that portion of the earth's surface on which they grew. So the productions of the human mind, be they classed with weeds or flowers, are indications of the age and the people giving birth to them.

In July 1832 a notice appeared in the *Virginia Herald* advertising the sale of the "Llangollen Boarding School Establishment." Llangollen and John Lewis apparently succumbed to the poor economic conditions that plagued Virginia at that time. The place was sold—dirt cheap. He moved to Kentucky, near Frankfort, where the school was reestablished, retaining the same name.

Published August 11, 2001.

Hello! Hello!

LONG DISTANCE SERVICE IN FREDERICKSBURG IS A HUNDRED YEARS OLD.

W hen Fredericksburg got its first telephone service, there was great excitement. The newspaper even reported the number of calls made each day.

It was during the 1880s that the telephone established itself as an essential technology. Wires and poles crisscrossed cityscapes and intruded upon vistas across America, ushering in dramatic changes in daily human communications. But the telephone was somewhat late in getting to Fredericksburg. The first mention of telephonic communication in the local papers appears in the *Fredericksburg Star* on May 11, 1889.

> *Last Wednesday morning the wire of the Northern Neck Telephone Company reached this place and on Thursday put in working order, with headquarters at the Western Union Telegraph office. The line extends to Heathesville, in Northumberland County. The main line takes in King George C.H., Oak Grove, Warsaw and other places.*

The first telephone call then, in or out of Fredericksburg, was placed on May 8, 1889.

The *Star*'s editor had a long conversation with the president of the company, William A. Jones, and congratulations and forecasts of financial success and rapid expansion were extended to the enterprise and to Mr. Jones. The connection involved eighty-five miles of line that had been stretched over the previous ten months. News of the line's completion was phoned to Fredericksburg, and then telegraphed to Mr. Jones's boss in Baltimore, showing that the two systems were used in combination. The *Star*'s report congratulated the company and lauded the achievement, "which places one of the richest and most important

This undated view of Caroline Street in Fredericksburg looks south from William Street and depicts telephone poles installed on the west side of the road. The alley to Market Square is visible at the far right. The presence and design of the automobiles indicate that the photo was taken years after the inception of phone service, yet the image provides a sense of how downtown appeared in the beginning of the twentieth century. Familiar surviving buildings include 914, 908, 904 and 826 Caroline Street. *Courtesy of the Library of Virginia.*

agricultural sections of Virginia in speedy communication with the outside world."

In March 1891 the *Fredericksburg Star* reported several of the city's civic and business leaders met in the office of the Fredericksburg Manufacturing Company to organize the formation of a local telephone company. The purpose of the meeting was to devise a plan to get a telephone exchange in Fredericksburg and to establish connections with surrounding areas, as well as White Hall, Vaucluse and other area gold mines.

Various committees were formed under the chairmanship of Isaac Hirsh. Hirsh operated a dry goods, millinery and ladies' ready-to-wear business on Main Street, as Caroline Street was then known. There was a sense that Fredericksburg was being left behind in this important communications development.

> *In the lower part of Virginia, in the valley and in the piedmont sections the counties have taken stock and subscribed liberally and the investment*

has paid handsomely. The company will go to work in earnest at once. Don't let it fail. Certain parties in the north have indicated their desire to become stockholders. This is a move in line with progress and development and it will succeed.

Local newspapers reported nothing on the subject for the next few years. In March 1895, the city council received a proposal from the Occoquan and Woodbridge Telephone Company seeking the privilege to erect poles and wires on the streets of the city, and to establish an exchange here. There was some opposition to passing this resolution because some members thought the issue should be tabled and given further consideration, but the franchise was awarded on a recorded vote of six in favor and three against. The resolution contained some interesting conditions and specifications: a performance clause stipulated that the project had to be complete and functional in six months.

The *Star* reported:

> *Poles had to be smoothly dressed and neatly painted; the company could not erect any poles in front of a house without permission of the owner; the price of annual telephone rentals would be fixed at $25 for businesses, shops and offices, and $18 for residences. Finally, exercising their negotiating prowess, the council stipulated that the company furnish, free of charge, one telephone for the mayor's office.*

The city of Fredericksburg would finally have a telephone system, seventeen years after the nation's first exchange was opened in New Haven, Connecticut, in 1878; ten years after the formation of AT&T in 1885; three years after long distance service was initiated between New York and Chicago in 1892; and one year after Bell's patent expired and the industry was opened up to competition in 1894.

Just one month after the city sealed its deal with Occoquan and Woodbridge, a representative of Bell Telephone contacted the city council. Mr. R.B. Rood, Richmond manager of the Bell Telephone System, visited Fredericksburg just a few days before the Occoquan and Woodbridge Company was to commence service. The company did not have exclusive rights and Mr. Rood was testing the waters, contacting local business leaders and exploring the feasibility of Bell Telephone setting up a local system. A reporter noted:

> *His terms are liberal, and he proposes to give first class service and charge $20 per year, payable quarterly for the use of the phones. In order to start*

> *the business he must have 25 or 30 subscribers. This number he did not get, as a number of our merchants have already made arrangements with the Occoquan and Woodbridge Telephone Company.*

Mr. Rood told the *Star* that he would submit a report to his company about the situation in Fredericksburg.

On April 30, 1895, the *Star* reported that the construction superintendent with Occoquan and Woodbridge was "busily engaged with a force of hands putting up poles and stretching the wires of the system." The central office was being "fitted up" and the whole system was scheduled to be serving all subscribers by mid-May. The central office, or exchange, is presumed to have remained at the Western Union telegraph office, where the city's first call was received in 1889. According to Sanborn Fire Insurance maps, the telegraph office was located at the southeast corner of Hanover and Main in both 1896 and 1902.

Apparently that completion forecast was correct. An article appearing in the *Daily Star* on May 17 conveys in colorful and effusive detail the excitement and enthusiasm one reporter had for the telephone. It was captioned "The Telephone: Its Many Advantages to Our Citizens." The writer announced that the system was up and running, and proving a great convenience to the business community. He predicted that the list of subscribers would double in no time.

Our scribe relates the story of a

> *Commerce Street merchant that had received two messages from the steamboat wharf, two from the* [railroad] *depot, one from the lower end of town and one from the National Boulevard, all of which had been attended to in less time than it would have taken him to send his wagon to the steamboat. He wouldn't be without the telephone for four times its present cost.*

Our reporter witnessed a bit of drama in what surely must have been one of the first (if not the first) telephone altercation to unfold in Fredericksburg.

> *While* [the merchant was] *conversing with us there was a telephone call, and after a few minutes spent at the instrument, in which the parties seemed to be engaged in a heated discussion, there flew across the line to the party at the other end, "You're a liar. What's that you say?" And the words were repeated. "You wouldn't use that language if I was near you," the downtown man replied. "Well come and see if I wont" was the reply.*

"All right, I'll be up there in a few minutes and see if you will repeat that language."

In a short time in walked the belligerent citizen from Darbytown, wanting to know what the Commerce Street merchant meant by this language. "Well," replied our uptown friend, "I was too hasty and I found I was mistaken, and called to you to correct it, but found you were already gone. I beg your pardon." And soon the two were laughing over the incident as though nothing had happened, another illustration of the advantages of the telephone. For if these two well known citizens had been near each other when their blood was up, there would have been a knockdown and drag out. But as it was there was time for them to cool off.

O Yes, the telephone is a great thing, and we hope there's millions in it for its projectors.

The *Daily Star* published a list of subscribers beginning on May 17, 1895. Locations and telephone subscribers were listed along with their one- or two-digit numbers. There were a total of forty-two numbers on that first list. Approximately fifteen were residences and the rest were businesses, professional offices or government. To reach the post office you would dial "1."

People were unfamiliar with the technology and the telephone was sometimes explained in stark elementary terms that seem ludicrous today. An early advertisement published by the Telephone Company of Canada explained that the telephone

> *uses no moving machinery, is perfectly clean and always ready. No skill is required by the users. The instrument is neat and portable, and an ornament to any room or office. The telephone conveys the quality of the voice, so that the person speaking can be recognized at the other end of the line. It transmits names, figures, foreign words, or plain English with equal facility, and as fast as the person speaking would ordinarily converse with one in the same room.*

Another subscriber list was published on September 20, beneath a caption reading "Fredericksburg Telephone Exchange. Hello! Hello! The lowest rates in Virginia." The number of phones in service was now fifty-nine. A total of seventeen new telephones had been added to the system, signifying 40 percent growth in three months.

The newspapers also began running little briefs about the number of calls that were being handled by the exchange each day. Sometimes these reports contained enlightening comments, such as the one appearing in the *Daily*

Star on September 28, 1895. It demonstrates that local politicos and their foot soldiers quickly utilized this powerful new organizing tool:

> *The calls through the central office of the telephone system for the past three days are as follows: Wednesday 188, Thursday 203, and Friday 226. Some of those who were in the minority at last night's mass meeting* [political rally] *intimated that the increase in Thursday's and Friday's calls was caused by the "machine" drumming up the henchmen. We can testify that the drumming up was very successfully done, but by what means it was accomplished we will not attempt to say.*

There are indications that a single operator worked at the exchange making connections in that first year of service. The paper characterized Miss India Scaggs as a "busy young lady," making 867 connections in four days, closing out the month of September.

A directory was published in the newspaper again in April 1896 listing sixty-four numbers, an increase of five from the previous listing.

In February 1897 the Occoqaun and Woodbridge Telephone Company was bought out by the Rappahannock, Fredericksburg and Piedmont Telephone Company, a newly chartered corporation headed up by local business and civic leaders. The company's president was the mayor of Fredericksburg, W. Seymour White (White was also part owner of the *Daily Star*). M.G. Willis, city councilman and future mayor, was vice-president. H.F. Crismond was secretary and E.D. Cole, a longtime councilman who was defeated in May's election, was treasurer. The company's directors were tight lipped about the amount of stock sold, but the *Star* reported that "enough had been subscribed for to put the plant on a sound basis."

On July 31, 1897, the *Daily Star* reported on a squabble between the city council and lawyers for AT&T, then a subsidiary of American Bell Telephone. Back in May 1895 the council gave AT&T the right of way through the streets of Fredericksburg for the purpose of installing long-distance lines. This was AT&T's main business. The company's important Washington to Norfolk line was almost completed, and it was requesting final agreement of the specific route through the city limits that its lines would take. The city council presumably had been stalling for fear that the monopoly, once established here, would compete with the home company for local business.

Incidentally, local magistrate S.J. Quinn, writing in 1908, characterized all the early service as "defective."

The corporate officers of the Rappahannock, Fredericksburg and Piedmont Telephone Company, and the elected leaders of Fredericksburg were, in part, one and the same. AT&T assured the council that neither they nor their parent company, American Bell, were interested in the local exchange. But it was AT&T's standing policy to deny long-distance access to independent companies.

The fact that Fredericksburg's political leadership had a direct stake in the local phone business notwithstanding, the 1890s was an era of strong antitrust sentiment, when numerous social and economic ills were blamed on the excesses of huge corporations. Across America, independent telephone companies were setting themselves apart as "Home" telephone companies, employing local capital and labor and trying to grow prosperity in their own backyard. Communities across America were reluctant to have local telephone service controlled by rapacious monopolies.

On July 30, 1897, one day before it reported the squabble between the city council and AT&T, the *Star* published a report about the Common Council of Richmond's defeat of an ordinance that would have allowed AT&T to come into and through that city. The caption read, "Council Did Right. People Commend its Action on Long Distance Ordinance. . . Richmond Will Be Passed By. This is the First Refusal the Company Has Ever Had."

The newswriter began,

> *The defeat of the measure met with general approval. This is not because the people of Richmond are not progressive and public spirited, but because they did not feel that the company should be permitted to come in their midst and do a local business in opposition to the home enterprise and capital without being subjected to the same restrictions and conditions.*

An AT&T official downplayed the defeat. He said:

> *Our line is completed from Norfolk to Yellow Tavern (north of Richmond) passing Richmond on the west and crossing the James River near the Belt Line Bridge. This we were compelled to do because the city of Richmond delayed so long in granting consent to our connecting Richmond with the long distance system.*

The *Star* article summarized:

> *The papers and people generally approve of the action of Richmond's council in refusing to surrender to the telephone trust, as the people here [in Fredericksburg] will approve of the action of the City Council when they know the facts.*

Don't Worry About the Weather

The weather seldom suits us. In winter it is too cold, and the snow is so disagreeable. In the spring the wind blows too much; in the summer the sun is too hot; and in the fall it rains most of the time.

But why worry about it? Install a Bell telephone, and you are immediately independent of the weather.

THE CHESAPEAKE AND POTOMAC
TELEPHONE COMPANY
OF VIRGINIA
M. T. GAULDIN, Local Manager

Tel. 9000   **Fredericksburg**

Chesapeake and Potomac Telephone Company newspaper ad. *Courtesy of* the Daily Star, *1913.*

==FOR==

Best Treatment. Best Values. Best Quality, Best Measure, Best Liquors of all kinds

But local resistance to the trusts would eventually collapse. In September 1903 the Rappahannock, Fredericksburg and Piedmont Telephone Company sold out to Southern Bell Telephone and Telegraph. Southern Bell had the locals over a barrel, dangling the carrot of access to a nationwide long-distance infrastructure. The council, by unanimous vote, granted the company the franchise.

Southern Bell would connect the city with points all over the country via its long-distance line, ushering in a new era of communications to the little city on the Rappahannock. Mr. Fairfax E. Montague, representing Southern Bell, said that the local system would be rehabilitated "and put in good order at once, and that Fredericksburg would have as good telephone service as any city in the country."

Southern Bell Telephone took charge about November 1. One month later L.N. Jeter of Richmond, a foreman with the company, arrived in town to supervise putting up the new "plant." Most of the material had arrived, as well as a large force of hands.

The *Star* reported:

> *New poles will be put up, new wires strung, new instruments placed, and everything connected with the plant will be entirely new. The instruments will be of the latest improved type, and will have the long distance connection.*

Local company manager W.T. Jones stated that the "plant would be completed in about sixty days."

In January 1904 workmen digging deep holes for large telephone poles stumbled onto a surprise on Princess Anne Street, near Saint Georges Episcopal Church. A number of human bones, teeth and other remains were discovered. There was much speculation and questioning about why people had been buried in a spot that is a public street, and about who they were. The *Star* included a curious remark, stating, "It is said by some of the best informed of our citizens as to the past, that it was a frequent occurrence for a body to be buried in the street."

On March 18, 1904, the *Star* announced that Southern Bell Telephone had completed its new plant, and that customers were very pleased with the new system.

> *Long distance telephone connection can now be given to any point where Bell instruments are used, from any residence or business telephone in the city. Fredericksburg is to be congratulated on having a telephone system as up to date as any in the country.*

Sometimes it is best to surrender and move on.

Published March 20, 2004.

Voodoo and Conjuration

AFRICAN TRADITIONS OF MYSTIC EMPOWERMENT

The practice of conjuration was carried out by quite a few," said Marrinda Jane Singleton, a former slave from Norfolk, Virginia, born in 1840 and interviewed for the Virginia Negro Studies Project—a part of the Federal Writers' Project—around 1937. She continued:

> *The negroes who were from the Indies and other islands were greatly responsible for these teachings. The brewin' of certain concoctions composed of roots, herbs and scraps of cloth with certain fowl feathers was believed to work charms or spells on the persons desired . . . They believed that [if] herbs or roots of certain types were placed where the victim would walk over 'em, he would become deathly ill soon after and perhaps die of the spell if it was not removed.*

Voodoo and hoodoo, or conjuration, were powerful belief systems influencing the thoughts and behaviors of blacks throughout the slaveholding western world. Voodoo is more closely associated with Haiti and Louisiana—New Orleans especially. Hoodoo flourished among blacks throughout the American South. Distinctions between the two overlapping systems are easily blurred, but hoodoo "doctoring" was tailored more toward protection or problem solving at the everyday level through casting spells, concocting potions or divination, whereas voodoo took the form of a religion, with considerable attention given to ritualized and systematic communication with, and petitioning of, spirits.

The word *voodoo* originates from *vodun*, meaning "god," or "spirit," in the language spoken by the Fon people of Benin (formerly Dahomey), West Africa. This empowering, complex belief system was brought to New Orleans by slaves transported from Haiti (then called Saint Domingue)

The use of images to cast spells is fundamental to voodoo and hoodoo. The most widely recognized is the voodoo doll. *Courtesy of Eva Kamieniak.*

by the French colonials fleeing the carnage and horrors of the Haitian revolution. Conflict erupted in the years between 1791 and 1804 between slaves, *affranchise* and French troops and civilians. The *affranchise* were free mulattoes, often wealthy and slaveholding, who aspired to the higher levels of French colonial society. They were denied full participation in white society and were generally despised by the slave classes.

The Haitian revolt was the long, ripening climax of a century's cruelty and injustice where approximately 500,000 African slaves toiled for about 32,000 European colonists and 24,000 *affranchise*. Fugitive slaves, known as Maroons, lived covertly in the mountainous interior of the island and often acted as voodoo priests, integrating and cementing the various tribal groups using shared spiritual traditions. Voodoo contributed organization and emotional strength to the rebels. The leadership and inspiration of voodoo priests was at least partly responsible for a massive slave uprising in 1791.

It was within these vicious power struggles in Haiti that the concept of the *zombie* developed. According to interpretation at the New Orleans Voodoo Museum, a person selected for *zombification* was given a potion prepared from plants and poison extracted from the blowfish. While the victim remained conscious, he was totally paralyzed. The victim was then buried alive, and after several hours he was exhumed and given an antidote. After this experience the victim was thought to have communicated with the dead. The primary purpose was to render the person docile and easily dominated by his master.

This is not to suggest that African mysticisms suddenly appeared in America with the arrival of Haitian slaves. Voodoo was well established in New Orleans by the mid-eighteenth century, and wherever and whenever slaves were brought to America their spiritual and magical traditions might become apparent.

In 1771 Peter Hansbrough of Stafford, Virginia, suspected his slave, who was named Sharper, of procuring poison from "a Negroe Doctor or Conjurer as they are Call'd." Hansborough obtained an arrest warrant from county justices and Sharper was apprehended and placed in the county jail. "Upon examination it appeared to the justices that said Sharper had attempted to procure poison from the doctor to destroy white people." Because of various delays affecting the trial, Sharper languished in the jail, and "was bit by the frost to such a degree that it commanded pity from every human heart." According to Handbrough's petition to the House of Burgesses (for compensation from the county for his lost slave) "the wound was so great that first his feet came off and then his legs grew worse until he died."

In the affairs of slaves, conjuration was crucial to obtaining justice when one slave sought revenge against another. Slave owners were adamant about protecting their property so consequences would be bad for a slave inflicting bodily injury against another. Therefore, malevolent spells and magic were often employed to settle scores.

One Virginia Negro Studies Project interview relates the recollections of Virginia Hayes Shepherd. Shepherd recounted the story told to her by her stepfather, who was a slave. An enemy put some substance on his horse, which got onto his buttocks and caused something like a boil. "After a few days it burst and live things came out of the boil and crawled on the floor. He thought he was conjured."

The world view supporting voodoo and related belief systems originates with West African animism and spirit worship. Ron Bodin, in *Voodoo Past and Present*, wrote:

> *In the West African view of things man lived and man died—that was natural. In the natural order of things the trees, the animals too, were born and died. Yet death was not seen as an end of life, for life was a continuum and after death man's spirit, his ghost, remained close by loved ones—caring, assisting and helping meet their needs. Since man had doubles, each animate and inanimate object in nature did too. This world of "spirit-doubles" was revered by the West African.*

This environment, rich in spirits, is dominated by a supreme god. In Haitian voodoo he is *Gran Met*, or "Great Master." His cosmic supremacy disallows him to trifle directly with human matters. Therefore the *loas*, or "sub-deities," are called upon by believers to act as intermediaries. Each *loa* has a name, a distinct personality and favorite foods, drinks and colors. Each type of *loa* possesses special powers and abilities.

There are three main groups of *loa*: the *Rada* are beneficent and most ancient, favoring the color white; the *Ghede* are bawdy and lewd, known for telling jokes and giving advice, and are represented by the colors black and purple; the *Petro*, symbolized by red, are protective, aggressive and possess strong magical powers.

Communication with ancestors and other departed souls is an important aspect of voodoo. Rites include prayer, song, drumming and dancing. Participants work themselves up into a trance, seeking to be possessed by the spirit. Possession is normal and good in the context of ceremony.

Popular depictions of voodoo often include human bones and skulls. Their uses or appearance are not intended to intimidate, or to suggest danger. They represent ancestors and serve to facilitate contact with spirits. Bones are considered to have magical qualities if they belonged to a *houngan* or a *mambo*, that is, a "priest" or "priestess." In Haitian cemeteries grave robbers are a persistent problem and extra measures are taken to ensure security.

The humfo altar at the New Orleans Voodoo Museum. It is described as a healing altar where petitioners needing divine intervention leave photos and offerings. *Courtesy of the author.*

Organic matter of all sorts is thought to have power in both voodoo and hoodoo superstition. Plant and animal material is used in a variety of ways, and in imaginative combinations, to protect, cast spells and effect changes. Voodooists have their gris-gris (pronounced "gree-gree") bags and juju; hoodoo doctors have charms, tricks and potions.

May Satterfield of Lynchburg, Virginia, also an informant for the Negro Studies Project, detailed a recipe for a concoction designed to bring good luck: "git some rat veins, wil' cherry blossoms, an' bile 'em togedder wid whiskey an' make bitters."

Informant John Spencer of King George, Virginia, recalled:

> *When one Negro became angry with another, he would bury in front of his enemy's house a bottle filled with pieces of snake, spiders, tadpoles, lizards and other curious substances, and the person expecting to be tricked would hang an old horseshoe outside of his door to break the spell.*

In voodoo, elements of Catholicism were woven into the rituals and devotional objects as a result of Spanish and French influence on slaves brought to the West Indies and South America. Candles, crosses, bells and

Skulls incorporated into an exhibit at the New Orleans Voodoo Museum. *Courtesy of the author.*

many, many images of saints are inextricably woven into the voodoo system. The blending of African beliefs with Roman Catholicism was a natural one in many respects because both the Catholic and animist traditions both rely upon divine intercessors—beings that can get the message to the supreme god. It also has been noted that Africans were drawn to the ornate decorative traditions of the church and its penchant for lavish ceremony.

Haitian slaves had to conceal their spiritual practices. Out of necessity, they substituted Catholic saints to assume the identities of various *loas*—those specialized sub-deities. Saint Patrick for instance corresponds to Damballah, the snake deity. The ancient African thunder god, Charingo, is represented through Saint Barbara, and Saint Peter is worshipped as Ogun, the iron god. African objects of worship could be hidden behind Catholic iconography, giving slaveholders the impression that their chattel was being Christianized, as they wanted.

In hoodoo there are no traces of Catholicism, suggesting that these practices, as seen throughout the black South, did not necessarily migrate and spread out from Louisiana, or evolve from the voodoo of Haiti. And Protestant Southern slaveholders, with their widespread contempt for the Roman Catholic Church, would never have tolerated the Catholic icons evident in New Orleans–style voodoo.

Throughout western slaveholding history there is the white dislike of Africanisms—those cultural practices that were African in origin. Africanisms tended to unnerve white slaveholders, who were perpetually uneasy about the possibility of uprising or plots. They did not want to see behaviors in their slaves that they could not understand.

Marrinda Jane Singleton, the former slave whose recollections were cited previously, commented on white loathing of the African occult and black reverence for it:

> *Such superstitions and practices caused so much confusion among the slaves, along wid fear dat the Marsters took steps to drive it out by severe punishment to those that took part in any way. This did not put an end to these practices. Many of us slaves feared de charm of witch craft more than de whippin' dat de Marster gave. They would keep their tiny bags of charms closely hidden under their clothes.*

It was destined that secrecy and concealment were to accompany these beliefs, which thrived where people thirsted for control and hungered for changed circumstances.

Published March 5, 2005.

The Pledge and the Brotherhood

HOW THE SONS OF TEMPERANCE CHAMPIONED SOBRIETY IN ANTEBELLUM FREDERICKSBURG

Into every society where alcohol is introduced—no matter the age, no matter the place—it follows that some percentage of the population will develop into problem drinkers.

In the history of this nation the heaviest drinking coincided with the early 1800s, with some estimates placing per capita consumption at over 7 gallons of pure alcohol in those years (compare with 2.46 gallons in 1990). Men, mostly, drank a lot and drank often and people generally did not question it.

In 1784 Dr. Benjamin Rush of Philadelphia wrote a farsighted and insightful tract called *An Inquiry into the Effects of Ardent Spirits on the Human Mind and Body*. Rush identified alcohol as a drug and an addictive agent and characterized chronic drunkenness as involuntary. He suggested that once the appetite for drinking took root, a person was powerless to resist and only total abstinence could arrest the problem. These ideas were revolutionary then and were probably difficult for most people to accept.

Concerned Americans, who were alarmed by the personal, social and economic ruination resulting from alcohol abuse, fought for change. By the 1830s there were several temperance organizations operating throughout the United States, experiencing varied levels of popularity and effectiveness. Early temperance organizations were primarily concerned with discouraging or banning distilled spirits, and for the most part they remained silent about the abuse of wine and beer. A person could be an "abstainer" but still use beer, wine or hard cider. There was a big distinction in many people's minds between distilled and fermented spirits.

That changed with a new generation of temperance men. When the American Temperance Union met in Saratoga, New York, in 1836, they voted to bring all alcoholic beverages under the ban of total abstinence.

A few years later, on September 29, 1842, a new breed of temperance organization was born, initiated by sixteen men at a place called Teetotalers Hall, in New York City. This organization would aim to "bind men by a closer tie, and to enlist their interests and affections more warmly and effectively than the old societies had done," according to an article published in the *Virginia Historical Register* in 1850. The organization was the Sons of Temperance. Its mission was to "shield us from the evils of intemperance; afford mutual assistance in case of sickness; and elevate our character as men." It was several things rolled into one: a mutual benefit society, a secret fraternal society, a temperance organization and most importantly, a support group, though that phrase was not generally used at the time. It was an idea that caught fire throughout America, and here too in Fredericksburg.

According to a prizewinning essay written by Sons of Temperance member Alexander Martin, there were 255,236 members nationwide in June 1850. Here in Virginia, the Sons numbered 245 in 1845. By January 1851 the Grand Division of Virginia counted 16,432 members.

The Sons of Temperance was successful, popular and influential because it did many things right. Its founders and members understood alcoholism better than any group had up to that time. One key to the Sons' success was the exceptional organizational scheme guiding its operation.

The Sons of Temperance operated at three levels, just like American government. There were constitutions created for the national, state and local organizations. The official name of the national body was the National Division of the Sons of Temperance of the United States. The national division granted charters to the state or territorial organizations, which were known as Grand Divisions. The Grand Divisions in turn enabled and chartered local divisions, which made applications for charter to the Grand Division. After meeting certain criteria and submitting a fee, a local division would be chartered and usually supervised by someone from the Grand Division to "train them in the usages of the order."

Local divisions were given a number corresponding to the nationwide sequence of their admittance. By 1850 there were at least three in operation locally: Mercer Division No. 67 and Spotswood Division No. 109 met in Fredericksburg. The Mount Hermon Division No. 348 was formed in Spotsylvania. The naming of Spotsylvania's division is especially interesting, being clever and symbolic. The Sons' national emblem was a triangle with words corresponding to each side: purity, fidelity and love. Old Testament scripture identifies Mount Hermon as a great landmark for the Israelites at Palestine's northern border with Lebanon. The mountain has three ascents situated like the angles of a triangle. From the numbering of the

This illustration depicts an idealized youth as characterized by the Sons of Temperance: strong, sober, alert and virtuous. Notice the triangle emblem on the urn to the left, and the symbolic objects decorating the oval border. *Courtesy of the Library of Congress.*

three divisions it is evident that it took a little time for a group to form in Spotsylvania.

In 1853 the Spotswood division had 135 contributing members. They met at "Temperance Hall, on Charlotte Street between Caroline and Princess Anne streets," according to a piece in the *Fredericksburg News.*

Two women, one offering wine and the other water, represent good and evil, sobriety and intemperance, in this 1850s print. A serpent is coiled around the base of the table, perhaps alluding to Proverbs 23:32: "At the last it [intemperance] bites like a serpent and stings like a viper." *Courtesy of the Library of Congress.*

The Mount Hermon division met every Saturday at 3:00 p.m., and at 2:30 p.m. in the winter months, possibly at the general store at the courthouse area, according to their published bylaws.

At all levels, the Sons of Temperance had an identical hierarchy of elected officers who carried out the various duties within the groups. A look at each office and its purpose provides insight into the organization and its time.

At the top was the most worthy patriarch. The MWP presided over meetings (or conventions if at the national or state level). He handled constitutional and procedural questions, appointed committees, adopted passwords, granted charters for subordinate divisions and performed a host of other duties.

The magniloquent title *most worthy patriarch* may have been a bit much, even by nineteenth-century standards. A reporter for the *Fredericksburg News*, covering the second-anniversary celebration of the Mercer Division in November 1849, commented on the speaker, the "grand worthy patriarch" of a Petersburg group, though the reporter did not get the title quite right. In a stroke of irony too good to be true, the speaker's name was Drinkard!

> *Mr. Drinkard, though apparently a very young man, was entitled "a Great Grand Patriarch." From this appellation we should judge he would have told us something that came under his observation about the time of the flood.*

Touché.

Next came the most worthy associate (MWA). He served as a kind of vice-president, offering counsel and assistance, and sitting in for the MWP in case of sickness or disability.

The most worthy scribe (MWS) was responsible for "keeping a correct record of the group's proceedings." This was probably the busiest office in the organization. At the national level it paid a five-hundred-dollar yearly salary. The scribe handled all correspondence between his division and other local divisions, the Grand Division and the National Division. He was responsible for an annual written report, for filling out certificates and calling special meetings concerned with financial appropriations. It was the scribe's duty to report to other local divisions within ten miles of its place of meeting the "name, occupation and residence of any person suspended, rejected or expelled from the division," according to the constitution.

The next officer was the treasurer, who would pay all orders drawn by the MWP. He received and held all division money, keeping account and issuing monthly statements.

The role of the conductor is perhaps the most telling in illustrating nineteenth-century sensibilities and social priorities. The conductor's role was to supervise and attend to matters of ritual and display. Pomp and pageantry was extremely important to nineteenth-century fraternal societies, and the Sons of Temperance were no exception. Among other things, the conductor ordered and arranged parade participants. A diary kept in the early 1850s by Jeremiah Harris, a Louisa County farmer and teacher, describes his encounter with the Sons as he arrived at the train depot in Elk Creek, Louisa County.

> *I reached* [my destination] *amidst the full tide of a large concourse, collecting to witness the imposing ceremonies of quite a rally of the Sons of Temperance, my progress . . . being seriously impeded by carriages and equestrians. The ceremonies consisted of marching and countermarching in order, displaying their regalia and other symbols of their order, till the time arrived for entering the house (church), when after singing and prayer, the large meeting was successfully addressed, . . .* [after which] *the whole company were invited to partake in a very plentiful and very nice collation that had been prepared under the especial supervision of some of the good ladies of the neighborhood.*

At meetings the conductor introduced individuals for initiation, introduced visitors and furnished them with proper regalia. He laid out the officers' regalia in preparation for meetings and put it away, usually into a special wardrobe, after the meetings. He also looked after other ceremonial objects.

One critic characterized the sons' displays, badges and regalia as "ostentatious displays and pompous farces, using *ad captandum* appliances to catch men's fancies."

Alexander Martin had an answer for this kind of criticism: "If it rescues a drunk we have done good work. Would you reject the whole system on a matter of taste?"

Finally, as a reminder that security was a concern then as now, every Sons of Temperance division appointed both an inside and outside sentinel.

> *It shall be the duty of the inside sentinel to attend the door—to admit none but members of the Order, and candidates for initiation. The outside sentinel shall guard the door outside, and keep off intruders.*

The Sons, being a secret society, maintained certain passwords and practices that it reserved for members only—a standard practice among fraternal societies, and one that lent an edge of exclusivity and distinction to membership.

This sheet music cover offers a rare glimpse at the sort of regalia Sons of Temperance members would have worn at gatherings, meetings and ceremonies. *Courtesy of the Library of*

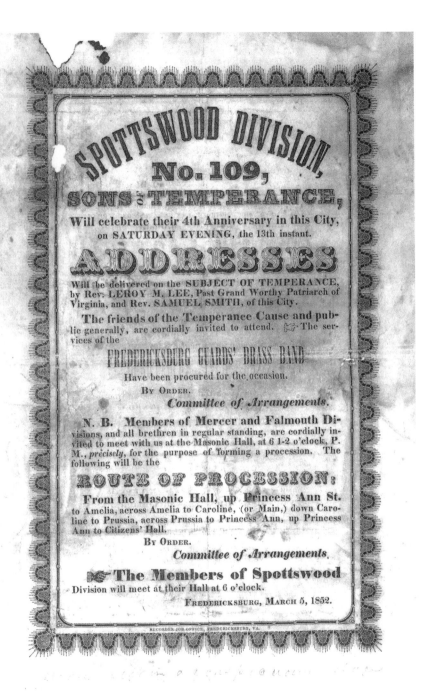

The Spotswood Division, Number 109, Sons of Temperance, announces its fourth anniversary celebration in this 1852 broadside. Music, speakers and a parade were planned. *Courtesy of the Virginia Historical Society, Richmond, Virginia.*

Who could join the Sons of Temperance? Eligibility required that a man be at least eighteen, pay a two-dollar fee, be of good moral character, not incapacitated in any way and have visible means of support.

To join the Sons, a candidate submitted his name, along with age, residence and business, in writing to the local division. The subject was then referred to three brothers for investigation, who reported back in writing at the next meeting. The candidate's name then was subjected to a ball ballot. If not more than four black balls appeared against him he was in. If four or more black balls were submitted, he had to wait six months before trying again.

Women did not belong to the Sons of Temperance, although their presence at public events was dearly valued. There are recurring hints in the documentation about the importance of the moral support of women.

The Daughters of Temperance was eventually formed, giving women an avenue for formal support of the cause. In January 1860 the *Fredericksburg Weekly Advertiser* reported that the Spotswood division "is now in possession of the Ladies Ritual, and those who may wish to have their names enrolled as Daughters of Temperance, are requested to be present next Monday night, or any Monday night following."

The Sons defended their exclusion of women, minors, the elderly, infirm and poor on the grounds of financial solvency, since the group was a mutual benefit society and paid a benefit to members, or survivors, upon illness, injury and death. In his 1851 essay Alexander Martin noted that "poverty as an obstacle is overcome for those who genuinely desire entrance to the order."

Martin painted his critics quixotic: "Our critics are crazed transcendentalists espousing indiscriminate charity. They grasp at shadows and would spend the energies of life in a discussion of moonbeams." In addition to the initiation fee the group charged dues of about six cents a week.

But expressing an egalitarian view, the closing verse of their installation song declared:

> *In Virtue only we behold*
> *The standard of our worth,*
> *Whatever station we may hold*
> *Among the sons of earth.*

For its time, the Sons of Temperance seemed to be a fairly open group (viewed in the context of mid nineteenth-century society) with a genuine desire to help afflicted drinkers from a fairly broad spectrum of society.

How did it work? How did the Sons of Temperance keep people sober? Central to the organization's principles was the "Pledge," appearing as article number two in the constitution at all organizational levels.

"No brother shall make, buy, sell or use as a beverage, any Spirituous or Malt Liquors, wine, or cider." The pledge was taken upon initiation to the group.

Those who violated the pledge were formally charged. A committee would take up the matter and vote to either reinstall or expel the offender. Brothers were expected to report violations. Failure to report could result in a one-dollar fine. The pledge breaker was also fined one dollar for the first offense and two for the second. A third offence resulted in certain expulsion, though in a nod to the tenacious and cunning nature of alcoholism, the Sons permitted reapplication after six months.

Much of their success was due to the weekly meetings and close associations between members struggling against a common problem. The training, discipline and regularity derived from these meetings helped members to resist temptation. Excellent communication between groups kept the subject of temperance continually in the public eye. In his essay, Alexander Martin reminded his readers:

> We present an undivided front . . . We act as with one spirit, and under one controlling influence, and so we learn not only how to obtain a victory but how to use it.

The sense of brotherhood and fellowship was crucial. When someone strayed or slipped, members pledged to find him and bring him back to "the peaceful and pleasant paths" from which he strayed. Sometimes search committees were formed to retrieve drunks and return them to the division rooms.

At a September 1850 meeting of Spotsylvania's Mount Hermon Division, following the quarterly election of officers, scribe Waller Holladay wrote, "much harmony and good feeling seemed to pervade the bosom of all the brothers present."

Closely related to brotherhood was the fellowship that was offered by the numerous special events organized by the Sons. A "Grand Temperance Excursion" was advertised in the *Fredericksburg News* in September 1849.

> The Sons of Temperance of Fredericksburg, having chartered the steamer Mary Washington, for an excursion to Tappahanock and back . . . take this opportunity of informing the citizens of Town and Country that the boat will leave the wharf at Fredericksburg . . . stopping for passengers at the Hop Yard, Port Royal and Smith's wharf.

Tickets were a dollar for gentlemen, fifty cents for ladies and twenty-five cents for children under twelve and servants. Confectionaries and refreshments were provided at moderate prices. Not surprisingly the Sons held a procession to the wharf prior to boarding for the excursion.

Another "Grand Excursion" advertised a few years later, and also aboard the *Mary Washington*, promoted the Fredericksburg Guards' Brass Band. That musical group was known to play at members' funerals. The advertisement promised that "the band will perform a number of beautiful Marches, Polkas, Galops and Waltzes. No liquor will be allowed on the boat under any circumstances. Perfect order will be preserved on board." Available refreshments included "ice creams, lemonade, soda water, oranges and confectionaries."

Another opportunity for fellowship presented itself in the quarterly meetings held by the state Grand Division. In April 1853 that meeting was held in Alexandria. The Rappahannock, Fredericksburg and Potomac (the RF&P) Railroad took Fredericksburg area members to that event for a fare of $3.50. The Grand Division also held a big annual meeting, according to the Sons' constitution.

Perhaps the most important events were the local rallies, where members of a few local divisions would gather—with regalia, badges and banners—to parade through the community. The destination would be a church or meeting hall, where one or more speakers would be expected to contrast, with colorful and convincing oratory, the misery of intemperance and the sweetness of sobriety.

One such rally is described by Waller Holladay in the September 1851 minute book of the Mount Hermon division, and takes place in Spotsylvania, presumably in the courthouse area.

> *The brethren to the number of 50 or 60, besides quite a large concourse of citizens, among whom were many ladies, met with us: all eager to participate in or to witness the ceremonies of the day.*
>
> *At about 12 o'clock the division together with all the members present from neighboring divisions, dressed in their regalia having formed a procession in front of Mr. Peakes store, marched under the conduct of Marshals appointed for the occasion to the church . . . The meeting was opened by prayer and singing. Brother Powell arose and presented on the part of the ladies a large and beautiful bible to the division which was received by Brother George B. Dillard in an appropriate speech. The meeting then adjourned . . . to partake in the abundant and elegant dinner . . . and having met again in the house were we greatly detained till a late hour by the speaker who addressed the meeting . . . This public demonstration will be of much good to the great cause to which our order is pledged.*

It was at events like these that members of the brotherhood found love, support and fellowship, and learned about new ways to live life.

When a brother of the Sons of Temperance died, the funeral ceremony would include these words:

> *Whatsoever in him was lovely and of good repute we give to the safekeeping of faithful memory—his errors we consign to the embrace of oblivion.*

It would be in the fulfillment of that idea that the successes of the Sons of Temperance could be measured.

Published July 30, 2005.

"Oh What Luxury!"

A CHRISTMAS PEEK AT A CHRISTMAS PAST

Looking at the Christmastime advertisements and reports of seasonal events in the newspapers, the word *holidays* appears to be used as often, if not more often, than the word *Christmas*. The newspapers I refer to are the *Daily Star* and the *Free Lance*, publishing in Fredericksburg in 1905. The word *holiday* was used interchangeably with *Christmas*. It is derived from the Old English *haligdaeg*: holy day.

I recently did a study of these newspapers, hoping to get a feel for the Christmas experience here in Fredericksburg, as it was a century ago, in both its material and spiritual aspects. Comparisons with the holiday as we know it today are informative and very insightful.

Looking first to the commercial side, holiday advertising then did not begin until December. Most merchants waited until the second week of the month before mentioning Christmas in their ads. The earliest reference to Christmas in a Fredericksburg newspaper advertisement (appearing in the two papers mentioned above in 1905) was on December 2, when Adams's Book Store began marketing books, novelties, picture frames and toys to "early purchasers of Christmas Goods." Adams carried an eclectic array of goods including musical instruments, wallpaper and bicycles.

Santa's career as a retail pitchman had barely gotten started. That year only one advertiser used an image of Santa—actually "good old St. Nic, everybody's friend," featured in an ad for J.B. Hall and Sons Stationers.

Some of the biggest advertisers included Kishpaughs Stationary, which used the Christmas countdown approach—"11 More Days to Xmas"—and so forth as the calendar dictated. Goolricks Modern Pharmacy advertised perfumes, candies, cigars and "Eastman Kodaks." Goolricks was a Main Street institution and a big draw with its bright lights and fancy cut-glass bottles on display.

Loewenson and Kaufman, "the old reliable jewelers," were marketing "Dainty and Appropriate Christmas Gifts." They offered rings, lockets, silver toilet pieces and "Ladies and Gentlemen's Watches in Endless profusion—$3.50 to $100."

Perhaps the biggest retail player in Fredericksburg was C.W. Jones, a department store of sorts, which opened in 1897 and used the most modern fixtures, display techniques and advertising schemes. They sold ladies' and children's tailor-made and ready-to-wear clothing, millinery, notions, rugs, luggage and other dry goods.

Their biggest competitor was likely the T.N. Brent Store, founded in the early 1880s. This thirty- by eighty-foot store sold fashionable dry goods on three floors. Their Christmas advertising stated that "this store will be open at night to give those a chance who wish to avoid the rush and those who are employed during the day."

Conspicuously absent in all the advertisements are stores' addresses and hours of operation, suggesting the level of familiarity that existed between the business community and the people in that era.

As the thermometer hit fifty degrees the Friday before Christmas, downtown Fredericksburg was crowded with people. Merchants and their assistants were kept busy from morning till night. Christmas turkeys were "much in evidence" with one merchant having over three hundred on display, with more being delivered throughout the day.

By 1905 it was increasingly clear that Christmas gift giving was an important aspect of the American economy. On December 12 the *Daily Star* reported that conservative estimates pegged spending on toys at eight million dollars nationwide.

> *This means about 60 cents apiece for the something like 13,000,000 of five- to twelve-year-old children. The children of no other country on the globe have anything like so lavish an average amount of money expended for toys for them. . . Verily, indeed, the lot of the American child has been cast in the richest sort of clover when it comes to toy getting and not a few other things in the bargain.*

The *Free Lance*, a few days later, carried a piece published in *Dun's Weekly Review of Trade* titled "Holiday Trade Booming." The article claimed:

> *Holiday trade has become the principal commercial feature, retail sales surpassing all records. Little machinery is idle, and the outlook for the future is brightened by several announcements of higher wage scales to become effective January 1.*

A Merry Christmas

Images of Santa Claus were pretty new among advertisers in Fredericksburg a century ago. One downtown merchant, J.B. Hall and Sons Stationers, promoted its goods with an image of "old St. Nic, everybody's friend." This Christmas postcard of 1907 seems to support that sentiment. *Courtesy of the author.*

On December 22 the same paper reported:

The giving and getting of presents is now more general than ever known. People generally are prosperous and money is more plentiful than for many years.

On the day after Christmas the *Daily Star* reported:

A perfect day [with] *no mishaps. The sun shone brightly, there was not a cloud in the sky, and the temperature ranged between 40 and 45. At an early hour the small boy was in evidence and the streets resounded with everything from the small to the huge cannon cracker* [miniature celebratory cannons also used on the Fourth of July]. *Later the streets were filled with beautifully gowned women and handsomely dressed men wending their way to Trinity and St. George's churches, where elaborate musical programs had been prepared. Many homes were bright with the loved ones who had come to spend Xmas. There was nothing to mar the pleasure of the day. There was not the usual dissipation (excessive drinking) incident to Xmas and not an accident occurred.*

There were however "Xmas Week Accidents." Fireworks were a customary part of the season's celebration. John Carter, "a student at Fredericksburg College, had a firecracker to explode in his hand, which injured his right eye." In Richmond, an extremely naughty boy

dropped a lighted match into the show window of Ungens Confectionary Store, on Main Street, which contained fireworks, and great excitement ensued. The windows were shattered and skyrockets cleared the store of people.

The store caught fire but the fire department was able to extinguish the blaze.

Lastly a fatal explosion occurred in Gloucester County when two boys found a can containing gunpowder. They thought it was dirt and used it to set a Roman candle upright. When the fuse was lit the can exploded. One of the boys did not survive his injuries.

A popular Christmas celebration of the time was the "Christmas tree," not the evergreen, but an event. They usually took place at churches for the benefit of children sometime before or after Christmas Day. Christmas trees usually included musical programs, pageants, entertainment, gifts of toys, treats and other fun for the children.

Under the caption "Beautiful Charity," the *Free Lance*, on December 30, described the Christmas tree put on by the ladies of the City Mission and the Elks for "the poor children of the city." It was hosted in the Saint George's lecture room. "Eighty-five children were entertained receiving candy apples and toys." There was a musical program followed by prayer. "Santa Claus was present in his sleigh and delighted the little ones who came forward each in turn to receive their candy from his hands."

Reports of Christmas trees held at area churches were numerous throughout the days surrounding the holiday. A dispatch from Spotsylvania dated December 27 paints this picture:

> *The Christmas holiday is passing very pleasantly hereabouts. Family reunions, Christmas trees, hunting and noise, the usual concomitants of the joyous season have been in strong evidence with us the present week.*

And then, as now, there were those people left behind by the joys of Christmas. A tragic revelation in the *Free Lance* of December 30 tells of a shoemaker living on Princess Anne Street who attempted suicide by shooting himself with a pistol above the right ear. The man was described as a cripple.

> *He was in bed with his small son when the act was committed. He has been a cripple for years and has been in such bad health that it has impaired his mind. His condition is serious.*

A doctor rendered aid but the bullet remained lodged in his skull.

Perhaps Christmas is mostly about contentment—of body and soul— through giving and receiving, through watching, listening and reflecting.

Published in one of the newspapers was a reprinted tale set in the English countryside during some unspecified Christmas season. A humble curate traveling by foot through the most miserable cold and rainy weather came upon an aged woman, who was weary and soaked to the bone. She pleaded with the clergyman for a trifle that she might get lodging for the night and some relief from her suffering. Being broke, the clergyman could not accommodate her request. But neither could he leave her on the road. He brought her home to his rooming house where his landlady had readied a table and a fire in the curate's room. The old woman, her clothes streaming water and her boots clotted with mud, was offered a seat in an easy chair by the fire where she was served hot toast and tea. Some moments passed in silence, when she suddenly burst into tears, and exclaimed, "Oh what Luxury!"

Published December 24, 2005.

On the Road

In the beginning of the twentieth century was the automobile, and the automobile was with America. And the automobile would come to define America—only America did not yet know it.

Who was the first citizen of Fredericksburg to own an automobile? That information can be found in the "Newsy Nuggets" section of the April 16, 1907 *Free Lance*, where "Many Minor Matters Merely Mentioned" showcased local briefs and press releases in a tumbling, captionless format.

> *Mr. Spotswood Foster, electrician at the Rappahannock Electric Light Plant, is the owner of an automobile, and attracted much attention as the machine sped along our streets Tuesday morning. It is the first one here owned by a citizen of Fredericksburg.*

While our reporter did get the who, what, where and when of the thing (but not the why), I—from my twenty-first-century, hindsighted perch— would have enjoyed more details. It is likely that most people living in 1907 could never have imagined how ubiquitous and universally influential the automobile would become. Thus the editor that day, almost a century ago, relegated the event to "minor matters."

By 1907 automobiles were becoming increasingly numerous in the United States. Fredericksburg was late in having its first car brought into town. In small-town America especially, during those first years of the century, having an automobile pass through town was a big deal. People would stop work, children would duck out of school and just about everyone would line the roads to get a look at these new machines. Local officials would be apt to extend formal greetings to the "automobilists." People would eagerly line up for rides.

Animal-powered conveyances were once the norm, as can be seen in this photo (circa 1901) of Caroline Street at its intersection with George Street. Goolrick's Modern Pharmacy, a Fredericksburg institution, is still in business. *Courtesy of the Rappahannock Regional Heritage Center.*

A view of the Caroline Street intersection with George Street after Fredericksburg entered the automobile age. *Courtesy of the Rappahannock Regional Heritage Center.*

The May 8, 1908 issue of the *Northern Neck News*, published in Warsaw, reported from Farnham in Northumberland County:

> *The sound of the "Automobile" has been heard in our village this week. Several of our school boys and girls had the pleasure of a ride, and were delighted with the speed of this "horseless" carriage.*

The big and oft-debated questions of the time were whether this new form of transportation was just a rich man's toy, good only for local travel in cities and towns, or a revolutionary new mode of transportation that would shrink distances and drastically change the way Americans lived their lives.

Here in Virginia the advent of the automobile made enough of an impression by 1902 that the General Assembly approved its first act regulating automobiles on December 20 of that year. The language and spirit of the legislation provides valuable insight into the skepticism and trepidation people felt toward the new machines.

The first paragraph of the Act to Regulate the Running of Automobiles sets a speed limit of fifteen miles per hour for any motorized conveyance operated on any "public highway, avenue, street or alley of any city in the State of Virginia." Riders on horseback and all animal-drawn vehicles had right of way and first consideration. If signaled to do so by any rider, the operator of an auto had to bring his machine to a full stop.

A roadster waits for a horse-drawn wagon to pass on a narrow country road near Liberty, New York. This photo, thought to have been taken in 1912, is an excellent illustration of the horses' waning supremacy concerning the rules of the road. *Courtesy of the Library of Congress.*

When a motorist was attempting to overtake a horse and rider or a horse-drawn vehicle stopped at the side of the road, he was obligated to sound a "bell or gong" and to pass at a rate of speed not to exceed four miles per hour. "The driver . . . shall in all cases use due diligence and care not to frighten the horse or horses."

Underscoring the General Assembly's apparent intention to safeguard the status quo (animal-powered conveyances), violators of the provisions of the 1902 act were subject to fines up to one hundred dollars. Their vehicles could be impounded and sold at auction.

In July 1907, three months after Mr. Spotswood Foster took delivery of his car, the city council noted that there was no automobile regulation in the city, and the ordinance committee was charged with preparing one.

Later that same month the mayor and the common council adopted as the law of the city the act of the General Assembly approved March 17, 1906, and titled an "Act to Regulate the Running of Automobiles, Locomobiles and Other Vehicles and Conveyances Whose Motive Power is Other than Animals." This was an expanded version of the 1902 law that addressed safety and accountability issues pertaining to the ownership and operation of automobiles.

This act gave birth to our familiar system of automobile registration, required safety equipment and rules of the road. Among the key aspects:

Every owner of a machine shall register the same by making application to the Secretary of the Commonwealth. The secretary then delivered a number plate four inches in height displaying a unique set of Arabic numbers followed by the letters *VA*. "This plate must always be in evidence on the rear of the machine." The fee was two dollars.

Speed limits within the corporate boundaries of a city or town were set at twelve miles an hour and fifteen outside. Drivers were expected to slow down going around curves, down sharp declines, at intersections and crossroads, going over the crest of hills and while passing other vehicles or riders.

Looking out for horses and their drivers and riders, the law stated:

> *If any horse ridden or driven in an opposite direction to that which the machine is traveling gives evidence of fright, then the duty of the driver shall be the same as if he had been signaled* [to stop] *by the rider of the horse or the occupant of the* [horse drawn] *vehicle.*

Additionally every machine was required to have a lock and key to prevent it from being "set in motion." It was illegal to leave a machine unattended with the key accessible.

Finally the act of 1906 required every machine to have "good and sufficient brakes and a suitable bell, horn or signal device." At least one white light, throwing a beam at least one hundred feet in the direction the automobile was going, was required equipment and had to be in use one hour after sunset to one hour before sunrise. The rear of the machine was required to have one red light that would effectively "illuminate the number tag on the rear."

But it was the automobile endurance races more than any other events of the times that were responsible for bringing motoring to the forefront of America's consciousness, and fortifying the foundation of a car-crazy society. Endurance runs were highly publicized distance races, sometimes with manufacturers sponsoring entries. Drivers and their automobiles would try to beat each other's time, traveling some great distance, usually between major cities.

This sport took a lot of spunk and resourcefulness. Roads were unimproved outside of cities and towns. Broken springs, snapped axles, busted drive chains and mud, mud and more mud, several feet deep at times, were commonplace. Gasoline had to be brought aboard, or delivered on the road if needed. Vehicles tanked up when they stopped in towns. The machines were cleaned and serviced. Drivers got food, drink and rest.

On March 7, 1908, the *Daily Star* covered a race from Philadelphia to Savannah, Georgia, between two thirty-horsepower touring machines—a

Prior to the widespread development of paved roads, automobiles often got mired in mud. *Courtesy of the Library of Congress.*

Pullman and a Studebaker. The drivers stopped in Fredericksburg for about two hours, having dinner at the Exchange Hotel and getting their machines washed, fueled and serviced.

Their approach to Fredericksburg was anything but smooth: "On Friday evening it was learned that the Pullman was 14 miles away, its stock of gasoline exhausted. A supply of gasoline was sent." On Saturday morning the same automobile was being drawn through the mud on the Warrenton Road, about three miles from Fredericksburg, by a team of six horses. Upon reaching Falmouth the team was detached and the Pullman, with flags flying, crossed the bridge and made a flamboyant entry into town. It then traveled down Main Street to the hotel.

Before departing Fredericksburg for Richmond the Pullman people, anticipating more impassable mud, hired a drag pulled by a team of four horses to accompany them. "This drag has in it 40 gallons of gasoline and the extra baggage taken from the car to lighten it." A big crowd turned out to witness the Pullman's departure.

And the Studebaker? It was twenty-five miles away when the Pullman was crossing the bridge into town. It was awaiting an order of gasoline. "It is probable that a team will be required to pull it through the mud, as in the case of the Pullman," the *Star* forecasted. But a later dispatch had the intrepid Studebaker seventeen miles from Fredericksburg, moving along on its own power.

On March 9 the *Star* updated its readers, disclosing that the Pullman had reached Richmond only one hour ahead of the Studebaker. The Pullman lost ground due to a snapped axle and its proclivity for getting caught in the muck.

Almost two years later, in May 1910, the *Star* covered a race involving twenty-six cars running from Washington to Richmond. This was a big social, economic and news event. A sizable party of Fredericksburg's business and civic leaders traveled to Orange, via the narrow gauge railroad, to meet the "Automobile Endurance Run Party, which passed there, and to inspect the machines." The Businessman's Association had other motivations as well, having to do with economic development. The association presented one Mr. Allen Potts, a key promoter of the race, with a "formal set of resolutions," some of which expressed disappointment that the race bypassed Fredericksburg. They explained to Mr. Potts why it would be a good idea to have their next event pass through their wonderful city (leaving behind few dollars).

In Orange, the machines came straggling in at varied intervals. The scheduled stay in that town was just thirty minutes. Roads between Orange and Washington were reported to be "fair," with most drivers running ahead of time.

Near Woodbury Forrest an accident occurred to one of the autos, the machine running into a tree and throwing out the entire party. A Mr. Daniel of Richmond was painfully, but not seriously, hurt.

Reporting the next day the *Star* explained that there were a few accidents and breakdowns as the cars struggled on to Richmond. There is no doubt that these were exciting events. The dispatch explained:

In one village the residents climbed to their housetops and cheered every car as it passed. In Louisa, Orange, Gordonsville and Culpepper a holiday was given to the school children, who lined every roadway over which the cars passed.

The development of a motoring culture presented Fredericksburg's City Council with an ample supply of new questions and situations needing attention. In May 1912, council minutes recorded that the ordinance committee recommended that no person under the age of eighteen be permitted to operate a motor vehicle. The law passed. A month later, three youths petitioned the council. J. Edward Tompkins, Emmett Colberth and Forrest Graves asked for immunity from the ordinance.

The minutes state:

> *The applicants are 16 years of age and* [revealing something of contemporary sensibilities] *a remarkable statement was made in the applications for this progressive age that neither of the three applicants smoked or drank.*

At their July meeting it was decided that permits to operate would be granted to the three boys, conditioned on certain restrictions, and subject to the continuing discretion of Mayor Rowe.

At the November 1914 council meeting, Dr. W.L. Bond, owner of Bond's Drugstore on Main and Commerce, "laid a bill on the table" claiming that two panes of glass were broken in the front window of his store by stones being thrown by passing automobiles. Apparently he felt local government should protect his property from such mishaps.

America as a nation on wheels, all sorts of wheels, had its detractors. An interesting glimpse into related problems is revealed in an ordinance proposed in council by one Colonel Cole sometime around 1910.

> *If any person shall run any handcart, wagon or wheelbarrow, or ride any bicycle or roller skates on the sidewalks of the city, or pavements surrounding any public monuments, he or she shall forfeit and pay not less than 50 cents, or not more than $5.*

It did not take long for local government to get creative in extracting new revenue streams from the automobile. The city council's finance committee in March 1912 proposed an ordinance imposing a license tax of twenty dollars per business on any building or garage housing automobiles for a fee. The same amount was levied on businesses using automobiles "for hire or use in transportation of persons for which a charge is made." Taxi businesses also paid an additional ten dollars per year for each additional vehicle.

The Fredericksburg city directories for the years 1910 and 1921 contain useful information underscoring the surge in automobility for that period. In 1910 there was one automobile dealer in town—the Fredericksburg Buggy Company. It advertised "Vehicles, Harness and Saddlery [and] The Famous Ford Automobiles." Notice the order in which the products were listed. The business was located at 407 and 409 Commerce (William) Street.

Also listed in the 1910 directory was George Gravatt. His business, George Gravatt Carriage Works, was a sizable facility incorporating a wood shop, storage, paint shop, dwelling and kitchen, located at 610, 612

An 1899 cartoon mourns the passing of the horse. *Courtesy of the Library of Congress.*

and 614 Princess Anne Street. This occupied, in part, the property of the present-day post office. The Sanborn Fire Insurance maps of 1907 depict the buildings in use at his business at that time.

On May 4, 1911, the *Daily Star* published a brief under the caption "Garage Now Open." Fredericksburg's first automobile repair shop was apparently a partnership between the Fredericksburg Buggy Company and Gravatt's Carriage Works.

> *The Fredericksburg Buggy Company has completed the equipment of its garage in the Gravatt building on Princess Anne Street. This is the first thoroughly equipped garage to be established in this city.*

It was mentioned that the building was repaired, painted, shelved and stocked, and an "expert machinist" was employed, "ready at all times to render aid to those needing assistance with their machines."

Fire insurance maps published in 1912 no longer refer to this group of buildings as the Gravatt Carriage Works. Number 614 Princess Anne, formerly the carriage works paint shop, is now referred to as a "garage."

At their January 1914 meeting city council considered an application to install the first underground gasoline tank in this city. Its capacity was 250 gallons. It is likely that the Princess Anne Street location alluded to in the council minutes was the location discussed above—the former Gravatt Carriage Works. The council's ordinance committee was also charged with developing a law "governing the handling and storing of gasoline in the city."

A third inspection of the fire insurance maps discloses that by 1919 all the buildings at the former Gravatt Carriage Works appear to be given over to the sales and service of automobiles. The community directory of 1921 lists 614–616 Princess Anne as home to the Virginia Motor Company, selling "Pleasure Cars and Trucks" including Chevrolet, Packard and Reo. There were five other major automobile dealers in Fredericksburg that year, all competing to deliver the magic of mobility to the people of the region.

The automobile had enabled people in Fredericksburg, and in the rest of America, to master distance as no other civilization in the history of the world ever had.

And with the passing of a century—a mere dust mote in the scheme of time—our automobiles, in some aspects, now master us.

Published June 24, 2006.

When Rubber Met Cinema

THE AUTOMOBILE, THE MOTION PICTURE AND PITTS'S FREDERICKSBURG DRIVE-IN THEATER

It was April 23, 1951, when the first drive-in picture show debuted in Fredericksburg. The feature attraction was director John Ford's majestic big-budget western *She Wore a Yellow Ribbon* starring John Wayne, with Joanne Dru and John Agar. The *Free-Lance Star* advertised "Pitts Drive-in Theater—a Car-full for a Dollar—Plus Tax—Shine or Shower—Route 1—Four Mile Fork." There were two shows nightly at 7:15 p.m. and 9:15 p.m. The flick was billed as "Drama that's Raw . . . Violent . . . Real."

The marriage of the car and the motion picture began in the early 1930s when a man named Richard Hollingshead Jr., while parked in the driveway of his Riverton, New Jersey, home, placed a Kodak 16mm projector on the hood of his vehicle. He focused it on a screen hung from a nearby tree, behind which played a radio. Subsequent experimentation involved varying screen sizes, projector throw lengths and the introduction of crude sound systems.

Then he designed a ramping system for parked cars so that the front of each car was pointed upwards and toward the movie screen. Drawings were produced and the concept patented, according to the book *The American Drive-In Movie Theater*, written and compiled by Don and Susan Sanders.

Matching Americans' love of cinema with their attachment to the personal convenience of the automobile was inarguably farsighted and brilliant. Hollingshead submitted the patent in August 1932 and in May 1933 "construction began on the world's first drive-in theater." It was located near Central Airport in Camden, New Jersey.

On June 6, 1933, Hollingshead's "Automobile Movie Theater" opened for business, to a packed lot, showing the second-run film *Wife Beware*, starring Adolphe Menjou.

The concept of the drive-in caught on like wildfire and by the time America entered World War II there were about a hundred drive-ins nationwide. But the war brought drive-in construction to an abrupt halt as Americans focused on the great task at hand, and steel (used in the superstructures supporting movie screens) was needed for more urgent purposes.

Now we return to Fredericksburg in the year 1950, and to the visions of State Senator Benjamin T. Pitts. Pitts was prominent locally in the pre- and postwar years. He was a Fredericksburg city councilman, a state senator representing the (then) twenty-sixth district and a philanthropist, community leader and founder of Pitts Enterprises Inc., which at one point owned thirty-six movie theaters and drive-ins operating in Virginia and one in Charlestown, West Virginia—thirty-seven theaters total.

Pitts was a nonfiction Horatio Alger story—writ local and writ large. The Fredericksburg Drive-in was his thirty-first theater, expanding a business empire he began in 1909 at age fifteen when he acquired the lease to the Old Fredericksburg Opera House on Caroline Street for $1 a night and purchased the projection equipment from the financially distressed owners. His start-up capital was $125—$75 of which was borrowed.

The local drive-in operated between Route 1 and Lafayette Boulevard. Its entrance was on Lafayette Boulevard just south of Fleming Street. "The long line of cars would stretch down Lafayette Boulevard and would block the entrance to our restaurant and to Fleming Street at night," said Pamelia Bettis, who at this writing still lives on Fleming Street with her husband John, adjacent to the tract where the drive-in was located. (The Bettises once operated the little restaurant fronting the drive-in site and presently trading as Grandma's Getaway.)

"People would open their car trunks and children would fill into them," Pamelia remembered. At some point the theater stopped charging by the carload and started charging by the head. The Bettises acquired their house in 1960—nine years after the drive-in began operation. As the screen was oriented northeast it directly faced their backyard. Parked theater patrons were just over their property line. John Bettis says he enjoyed sitting in his yard and watching movies. He was close enough to hear the sound from the car speakers in the back rows.

The drive-in was adjacent to the Virginians Theater, which was built in 1972 and demolished in March 2005. The two theaters operated simultaneously for about a dozen years. Pitts's Fredericksburg Drive-in was chartered by the state corporation commission in 1950, as was his drive-in in Culpepper. He also had drive-ins under construction in Orange and Manassas at that time and was planning to build seven more, according to a November 21, 1950 piece in the *Free Lance-Star*. It was the golden age for the drive-in theater and Pitts was in the game and out front.

Benjamin Pitts of Fredericksburg was a movie theater mogul—a real-life Horatio Alger protagonist. *Courtesy of the* Free Lance-Star.

The Fredericksburg Drive-in cost about $125,000 to build. To put that in perspective the annual median income for American families in 1951 was $3,709, according to census bureau tables. The *Free Lance-Star*, reporting on the theater's opening, stated that the screen was "made of solid steel and embedded with 50 yards of concrete." It was sixty-five feet high and fifty-five feet wide and was said to be engineered to withstand winds exceeding a hundred miles per hour.

The parking lot required $10,000 worth of crushed stone trucked in from Culpepper. The article described the facility in detail:

> *There are individual speakers for all cars, a concession stand that sells hotdogs hamburgers and such and also has speakers so you won't miss a tart bit of dialogue while munching on a ham and rye.*

A three-hundred-foot well was drilled to supply water to the site, modern restrooms were installed and the sound and projection equipment were said to be "the most up-to-date."

The article cited many reasons for the growing popularity of the drive-in at that time. You could hear the actors' lines after a joke, unlike in a movie house where the

> *bedlam breaks loose and you hear nothing thereafter for a few moments. If nobody chuckles in your car you hear the next line. It's good for families with babies. No baby sitter required, take the tike along. If it cries it won't disturb other movie goers. There's comfort and privacy. No standing up to let people by, no peering around milady's hat. You can control the volume of the speaker. You can smoke And—no chewing gum on the seat.*

Pitts's original concept for the Fredericksburg Drive-in included a fishing pond, a merry-go-round and a miniature train. Many drive-ins across the country installed multiple attractions, including miniature golf, and marketed themselves as family entertainment destinations. As best as can be determined, only the fishing pond was built.

Pamelia Bettis recalled that "there was a big pond on the side of the theater where people caught nice fish." The pond also spawned mosquitoes, which could sometimes subtract from the fun.

The *Richmond News Leader*, in a February 29, 1956 profile piece about Benjamin Pitts, described the senator as "a lean blue-eyed individual who stands 6 feet 1½ inches tall and weighs in at a fighting 172 pounds."

The senator, being interviewed, was asked about the implications of growing television viewership on the movie business. "Television has

John and Pamelia Bettis stand on their deck overlooking new construction at the site of the former Fredericksburg Drive-in Theater. The couple watched movies from their backyard on Fleming Street when the drive-in was operating. *Courtesy of the* Free Lance-Star.

helped the industry," he contended. "Hollywood has learned a good movie can draw people out of their living rooms and goes about making good movies."

> *His ten drive-ins, which represent investment of $750,000, provide one particular problem. People are forever driving off without unhooking the speaker from their car window. And he doesn't go for all these tales about overzealous necking at the dollar-a-car-load cinemas.*

You get the sense the reporter may have struck a raw nerve in that topic.

But the term "passion pit" was not whipped up out of thin air. The term was "well deserved" according to Jim Mann, retired associate managing editor at the *Free Lance-Star*, who moved to the area in 1952. In Fredericksburg, and across America in the 1950s, the drive-in was "the place" where you went on a date. Large groups of guys would pile into cars and head there as well. The drive-in was especially popular with high school students. There were only three high schools in the area at that time: James Monroe, Stafford and Spotsylvania.

"Those were much more innocent times," recalled Mann. "The most serious contact with the opposite sex took place at the drive-in." For the most part it would have consisted of necking and holding hands. Many a person who went there could not remember much about the movie.

Mann pointed out that "most young people then did not have their own car." You would have to negotiate for that with the folks—dad most likely. One can only imagine how many paternal interrogations took place when the destination was the drive-in.

One native Spotsylvanian, who characterized his upbringing as "sheltered," did not go there often but recalls people putting friends in the trunk to get in free. "It was considered a place to make out and 'polite girls' would not go there—they would lose their reputations." But that was an evaporating point of view as the '50s ran their course and graduated into the '60s.

Mann emphasized that "movies were the primary form of entertainment then. The Fredericksburg drive-in was truly an important part of growing up here."

Published December 16, 2006.

Policing the Corporation

EARLY LAW ENFORCEMENT IN THE CITY OF FREDERICKSBURG

In November 1781 Fredericksburg was incorporated as a separate jurisdiction, apart from Spotsylvania. In that year the General Assembly in Richmond passed an act making Fredericksburg a "body corporate and politic" and giving it "perpetual succession" and all the rights and liabilities of an independent political entity.

This law set up the democratically elected twelve-member town council, consisting then of a mayor, recorder, four aldermen and six common councilmen. The mayor, recorder and aldermen—or any four of them— had the sole power "to appoint a *serjeant*, who shall have the power of a sheriff, constables and other necessary officers of the court." *Serjeant* is the first appointed office mentioned in the statute, perhaps signifying its importance.

The enabling legislation established that the mayor, recorder and aldermen were also the justices of the peace. When originally formed, the boundaries of the town extended to the "low-water mark on the north-west side of the Rappahannock River, and a half mile without and around the other limits of the said town." The justices had jurisdiction over all cases originating within those limits.

Stepping back a moment to put the era in chronological perspective, Fredericksburg was incorporated in the sixth year of the commonwealth's independence, about a month after Cornwallis surrendered at Yorktown, eight months after the last state (Maryland) ratified the Articles of Confederation and six years before the states were united under a federal constitution.

Also in 1781, Spotsylvania's new courthouse was ready, the seat of government having been moved from Fredericksburg to the geographic center of the county, at the Po River on present-day Blockhouse Road.

This point in time seems an appropriate place to begin searching for information that might shed some light on early law enforcement in the city of Fredericksburg. Who were the first police and what were their responsibilities and experiences? What do we know about them and about the system under which they operated?

City council minutes indicate that Fredericksburg's first sergeant was John Legg. In March 1783 it was recorded that Legg was paid six pounds for services carried out the previous year. The duties of sergeant included collecting taxes, fees and fines; enforcing and collecting judgments; summoning litigants and public servants to court; and generally enforcing the decisions of the court. He was responsible for enforcing the laws of the commonwealth and the town.

Legg's duties also demanded that he ensure that firefighting efforts were organized, and equipment—such as leather buckets, ladders and hooks—were serviceable and in their proper place. These tools were sometimes borrowed and not returned in a timely manner. The danger in this speaks for itself.

The sergeant was superior to the constable and his job was seemingly a bit less gritty. But references to the constable's role are more revealing about Fredericksburg in that time. The constable's duties were conducted among the people and on the streets. It was a hands-on law enforcement position—more so than the sergeant's.

The first constable mentioned in council minutes is James Jarvis. In February 1783 accounts show Jarvis being paid in tobacco for the following services: summoning aldermen and council, "summoning 5 guards over the buckets," for whipping one "French John," for summoning witnesses to court, and for "whipping a white man per order Colo. McWilliams." This last task earned him the largest fee at ninety-five pounds of tobacco.

Sergeants and constables were paid by the service rendered—piece rate work you could say. It was a side job rather than a full-time situation. Both Legg and Jarvis, Fredericksburg's first sergeant and constable, did not remain in their posts for more than a couple of years' time. Nevertheless they have the distinction of being Fredericksburg's first cops. Both were attracted to more lucrative careers at the vendue, or public market, located approximately where the refurbished market square is today, between Princess Anne and Caroline Streets and adjacent to William Street.

Fredericksburg's council would ballot for a vendue master, often referred to as "VM" in the *Virginia Herald*. The vendue was part of the public market. High-value property and volume goods were auctioned here: imported products, cattle, sailing vessels, slaves and more. The real money was here. The vendue master was the auctioneer and collected commissions on the transactions. By all indications, it was a lucrative post.

"He stooped to pick up the scourge which his constable had refused to wield." A dramatized scene from *A Maid of Old Virginia* by William Sage. This photomechanical print was created by artist Victor Perard and published in 1915. *Courtesy of the Library of Congress.*

The VM had to pony up 8 percent of his commissions yearly to the chamberlain (treasurer) of the corporation—no doubt an important revenue stream for Fredericksburg. The council records give a sense that the law enforcement appointments (sergeant and constable), and those intended to regulate the public market (vendue master and clerk of the market) overlapped for the purpose of keeping order in the town. All four positions were official jobs of public authority.

According to an April 1810 report from the *Alexandria Gazette*, the public market in Alexandria, for example, needed policing during its busy hours to "keep order and prevent tumult and robbery of idle boys . . . preventing the assemblages and riotous play of boys of every description."

Though Jarvis was constable in 1784, sometime soon after that he was balloted into the vendue master's job by the town council. It was a step up. However, an entry in the council minutes dated January 1786 states, "James Jarvis late VM being dead John Legg appointed to fill the office." So Jarvis did not get to spend much time in that job—but Legg did.

There is a suggestion in council minutes that disagreement over payment for services performed as sergeant in 1783 caused Legg to separate from that office in May 1784. With his departure, council ordered Legg to present the list of "balances due the corporation" to John Richards, the corporation's second sergeant. Collecting sums due the corporation was Richards's job now.

In addition to keeping order in the streets, collecting taxes and fines, executing writs, warrants and attachments (property seizure resulting from judgments), carrying out the corporeal sentences of the court and generally enforcing all the laws of the corporation, the sergeant was responsible for managing public works, animal control, sanitation and fire prevention and control.

The Virginia Acts of the Assembly passed in 1792 specifically set the fees to be paid to constables. These itemized fees provide a glimpse into the nature of the constable's job as the eighteenth century waned. As there is now in existence a fledgling monetary system in the United States (the U.S. Mint having been created by Congress in 1792) fees are listed in dollars and cents.

	Dollars	Cents
For serving a warrant.	0	21
For summoning a witness.	0	10
For summoning a coroner's jury and witnesses.	1	05
For putting into the stocks.	0	21
For whipping a servant (to be paid by the owner and repaid by the servant).	0	21

	Dollars	Cents
For serving an execution or attachment (usually seizure of property), returnable before a justice.	0	21
For serving an attachment returnable to the county court against the estate of a debtor removing his effects out of the county.	0	63
For whipping a slave (to be paid by the overseer, if the slave is under an overseer, if not by the master).	0	21
For removing any person suspected to become chargeable to the county, (to be paid by the overseers of the poor) for every mile, the same for returning.	0	04

Joseph Berry was Fredericksburg's second constable, but its first regular "cop on the beat," in this writer's estimation. He served the city for about fifteen years and there is enough known about him to develop some acquaintance.

By January 1785 he was in the job. Council minutes order that "Joseph Berry attend to the keeping of good order in the streets." We know that his trade as a "Britishe maker offered small encouragement." "Britishe" probably refers to the "British warm," a short, heavy overcoat commonly worn by British military officers. As colonial rule had just recently been expelled at great cost and suffering, likely these garments were not too popular.

Because he was strapped financially, he was housing himself and his family somewhere within the courthouse, which was soon to undergo major repair. He needed a place for his family and himself to dwell. He could not afford a lot to build upon, or to pay someone the high rent for a house in town, so he obtained some scantling (dimensional lumber) and petitioned council. His petition is recorded in the March 21 minutes of council, reading in part:

> *That as the back of the Market house lott is unoccupied with any public buildings and as you are the trustee of the same he humbly prays leave to erect his small Fabrick on any part your worships would point out to him, and on what ground rent you would think reasonable.*

Berry also offered himself as a candidate for clerk of the market, promising to "discharge the office with fidelity—and will keep both the Market and the Room above always in decent order."

Berry's petition was considered by the board who

> *thought it reasonable considering that it would be useful in protecting and guarding the Market House, they do therefore permit the said Joseph*

Berry to erect a house on the side of the hill on the market lott and that whenever the representatives of the people in this Corporation should think it necessary to move the same that he shall do so.

George Weedon, the mayor, signed off on the petition.

There is no description of the constable's home. Perhaps it was a hall-parlor structure. Since it was built on leased ground, it was likely a rough and ephemeral dwelling. As the site is described as "the hill" I suspect his house fronted Princess Anne Street, where the present 1816 town hall is situated. In Berry's time the courthouse and market were on the Caroline Street side of the market square lots.

In 1797 his dwelling was still there, as council records reflect extension of his lease for another year, so we know the building stood for at least a dozen years. His rent for the lot at that time was three pounds per annum.

In the closing years of the eighteenth century Fredericksburg employed the number of constables it felt was needed, usually three or four. Others serving in this era included George Graves, Edward McDermott, George W.B. Spooner, Mordicai Mastin and William Berry, to name a few.

A constant challenge faced by the constables was ridding the streets of stray dogs and hogs—especially hogs. A 1798 list of tithable property lists 244 hogs in Fredericksburg. Also, there were hogs wandering in from Spotsylvania, like the ones belonging to Joshua Myers, who sued Joseph Berry and the corporation in the spring of 1797 after the constable shot some of his hogs.

The corporation settled because the law specified that loose hogs belonging to those who were not residents of Fredericksburg were to be "impounded," whereas hogs owned by residents could be shot. No doubt it was easier to shoot a hog than to impound one.

In 1785 council decided that dogs at large "were to be immediately killed by the constable." The public crier was to notify the citizens immediately, and the constable was ordered to "be attentive to this order under neglect liable to penalty."

This too was an ongoing problem. In June 1790 the *Virginia Herald* began a report:

Whereas sundry dreadful accidents have happened in and about this town, by mad dogs, it is ordered that all persons having dogs keep them tied up. And that Joseph Berry, John Atkinson and William Berry, constables, do kill any dog belonging to an inhabitant of this corporation any time they may find them running at large.

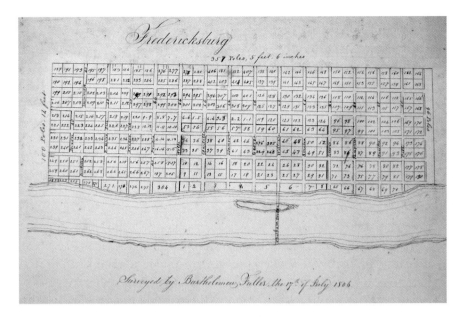

This plat of Fredericksburg, created in 1806 by Bartholomew Fuller, gives a sense of Fredericksburg's scope and the area that required patrolling. *Courtesy of the City of Fredericksburg Circuit Court.*

Notice was given by the town crier and by posting copies of the ordinance, which was published in the *Herald*, in conspicuous places.

In addition to the sergeant and constables, Fredericksburg organized and employed various forms of a "night watch," though this seems to have been an intermittent action with varied proposals popping up from time to time.

"It is the opinion of the board that a watch is absolutely necessary for the good order and safety of the town," states an entry in council minutes as early as 1783. "It should consist of a number of 8, 2 of which shall survey the streets of this town every night."

Mayor Fontaine Maury in 1796 appointed a committee "to employ 6 men in whom they can confide as a permanent guard or patrol for this town." The mayor also declared that the patrol would "carry about a subscription paper in order to get a sufficient amount of payment of such guard."

Property crimes, theft and burglary, were usually carried out in the depths of night. It also must be remembered that white people throughout the South were, and had been for scores of years, apprehensive about slave insurrections, which had from time to time been carried out, more often plotted and still more often rumored.

A patrol scheme of huge scope, relative to Fredericksburg's size (approximately fifteen hundred people enumerated in 1790), was organized by order of council and detailed in the *Virginia Herald* of August 19, 1806. White males between the ages of eighteen and forty-five were enumerated and organized into "classes" of six men, each having a captain. There were forty-one classes in total—subordinate and reporting to the magistrates of the town. They were to patrol the town from the hours of 10:00 p.m. to 4:00 a.m.

> *It was the duty of the magistrates to order out a patrol, or patrols, of the inhabitants of the town in rotation whenever they may deem it necessary.*

It is not clear how frequently this plan was implemented. The list of 246 names composing the 41 6-member patrols was published in the *Herald*.

Constable Joseph Berry died in 1800. Only this was published in the *Virginia Herald*: "Friday, July 18, 1800. DIED in this town Mr. Joseph Berry, constable."

The first use of the word *police* appears in council minutes, and in the *Virginia Herald*, on April 17, 1810. A committee was appointed to define the duties of the police officer. The minutes tell us:

> *It being the opinion of the council that the office of Police Officer and Clerk of the Market shall be combined. It is ordered that the said Officer be allowed the sum of $200. per annum.*
>
> *George W. Spooner is elected (by council) police officer in this corporation the present year.*

Spooner was a dry goods merchant whose cellar was robbed of candles, soap and "Continent rum" one spring night in 1792.

The committee appointed by council defined the duties, in part, of the police officer of the corporation. An abbreviated description states that the police officer had to see that the bylaws and ordinances of the corporation were carried out. More particularly, he had "to see that the constables do their duty on the Sabbath day keeping order in the streets."

He had to superintend the repair and improvement of the streets per direction of council; to see to it that the streets were not injured by "unauthorized removal of earth or gravel"; to ensure that the laws pertaining to nuisances and obstructions were strictly enforced.

Officer George W. Spooner was charged with inspecting the different wards, "and to see to it that ordinances respecting the prevention of accidental fire are judiciously attended to."

The police officer was responsible for reporting to the overseers of the poor every three months a list of "such poor persons that are likely to become chargeable to the corp., who may have settled within its limits during that period."

It was also the police officer's responsibility to "attend to the fire engine, having it worked at least once in every month, and taken to pieces and having it examined and oiled at least twice in one year." It was also his responsibility to ensure that the water hogsheads were filled and in good repair, and to report any problems concerning firefighting equipment to council.

In October 1807, less than three years prior to the council's instructions, a huge fire—stoked by a strong northwest wind—resulted in great loss and suffering for the people of Fredericksburg. That fire destroyed several square blocks of improvements and property. According to *The Fredericksburg Fire of 1807* by Edward Alvey Jr., no human life was lost.

It was further emphasized by the council that it was the duty of the constables, superintended by the police officer, "to prevent riotous or noisy conduct in the streets, on all occasions but particularly at night and on the Sabbath," and to assist the clerk of the market in the prevention of robberies, "tumulty" and to disperse the people from the market by 9:00 p.m.

As previously mentioned, Virginia's constables received set fees for particular duties performed. The General Assembly in 1807 passed legislation intended to check abuse by constables charging more than the allowable fees to citizens for such services as issuing warrants, subpoenas, attachments and others. Across the commonwealth, constables now had to post bond with their respective justices in sums ranging from five hundred to fifteen hundred dollars. This would expedite the recovery of any inappropriate or unjustified charges. Constables were also now subject to fines resulting from these abuses or errors.

Peace officers were salaried soon thereafter and a tax was levied on householders for that service.

During Spooner's tenure as police officer we know that Fredericksburg had some unknown number of "police houses" situated throughout the town. The number and physical appearance is unknown to this writer; however, in 1811 town council ordered them sold. Council minutes report that "John Chewning, a constable in this corporation made return that he had sold the watch houses for $1.75 which is paid to the chamberlain."

These police houses may have resembled booths, intended as a place of respite and relief from bad weather for officers patrolling the town. It is possible that whatever comfort and shelter they offered undercut conscientious patrol of the town by inviting goldbricking.

Concerning incarceration, corporeal punishment and restraint of prisoners, information from Fredericksburg's early years is sketchy. Upon ratification of a federal constitution, the states—Virginia included—set about revising their law codes. This work began in earnest in the 1790s. Some of the laws concerning capital sentencing and corporeal punishment and confinement prior to trial were modified or struck from state codes. And there were separate harsher codes applying to black and mulatto Virginians, free or slave.

Back in April 1785 council minutes noted a whipping post, stocks and a ducking stool were ordered. In January 1786 John Welsh was paid twelve pounds for "erecting public whipping post and stocks." The General Assembly allowed for the whipping of both blacks and whites through the end of the eighteenth century and well into the nineteenth century.

One Godlove Heiskell, a Fredericksburg coach maker and blacksmith, collected many payments from the town government for putting prisoners into irons—and for removing the irons from prisoners. Apparently not all restraints at that time operated with a lock and key and some required the knowledge and tools possessed by a blacksmith for putting them on and taking them off. They likely made use of a hammered rivet or pin.

Another fairly common occurrence was the arrest and confinement of unknown blacks, who were unable to produce free papers. Free blacks were required to possess documents demonstrating that they were not someone's property. Such papers usually took the form of a deed of emancipation, a copy of a will granting manumission or perhaps a bill of sale if a slave's freedom had been purchased. The constable would place an advertisement in the *Virginia Herald* announcing such apprehensions. It was a common occurrence. This example was published in July 1789:

> *Committed to the gaol of this corporation a mulatto fellow named TAYLOR, says he belongs to George Carpenter, overseer for Mr. Ball of Frederick County. He has three marks on his face, one over the left eye, one a little above the cheek, and one in the forehead. His owner is desired to pay charges and take him away. Joseph Berry, Gaoler.*

In 1796 Mayor Fontaine Maury signed off on a jail report that painted a bleak picture of that facility and emphasized the misfortune awaiting anyone unlucky enough to be remanded there. It reads in part:

> *The decayed and feeble state of the walls, daily crumbling to pieces Afford no security for the safekeeping of those who may be confined within them. Persons of all sorts put together in the same unwholesome and miserable*

situation. The effects would be fatal to the health and constitution of those confined—more than any sentence pronounced.

"By the Common Law Constables are conservators of the peace," wrote Joseph Mayo in his *Guide to Magistrates* published in Richmond in 1853. "They are important agents in the administration of the law, both civil and criminal, and as executive officers bear the same relation to Justices of the Peace."

Fredericksburg's earliest police performed a precarious job. They were shadowed always by discord, suffering, trouble and danger.

A Reminder of the Duties of Police Officers and Constables from the Mayor's Office
As Published in the Political Arena on October 20, 1841

The following edited memo from Mayor Benjamin Clark provides rich insight into nuisances, infractions and crimes occurring in Fredericksburg in the second quarter of the nineteenth century. The memo's intention was to make citizens aware of the responsibilities of the peace officers, specifically so "the citizens would know when the officers were in the discharge of their duties."

The notice begins:

> *For their information as police officers they are required to cause all nuisances, impediments and obstructions in the street to be removed; to give information to all owners of drays (carts) for hire which have not paid tax; to give information of the erection of any horse rack or trough which injures public property; to persons whose chimneys may catch fire in dry or windy weather, or for carrying fire through the streets without having the same properly secured.*
>
> *To give information about any person discharging firearms or crackers; against persons assembling and playing at any games or amusements, or throwing stones in any of the streets, or for flying kites, drawing any indecent figure or writing any indecent words in any public place; or for beating any drum after dark; for permitting a horse to run away while attached to any dray, and to give information against all persons who shall willfully strain any horse in the said corporation, or shall put any horse to any vehicle for the purpose of breaking such horse within the limits of the same.*
>
> *To give information against all persons who shall drive or ride on any of the footways, or roll any wheelbarrow on the same. To give information*

against all people who shall keep their shops open on Sunday. To prevent riotous and disorderly conduct in the street at all times, particularly at night and on the Sabbath.

As constables they are required to use their best endeavors to part all affrays that happen in their presence. They are required to suppress all unlawful and dangerous assemblies, to suppress all unlawful meetings of slaves, free Negroes and mulattoes. To apprehend such persons assembled and carry them before the justice of the peace. To apprehend slaves permitted to go at large and trade as free persons and all who profane the Sabbath day by trading with slaves.

Sheriffs, under-sheriffs (constables) and justices are made liable for failing upon information to cause them to be carried into effect, and that officers of Fredericksburg will use their best exertions to carry these laws into effect.

BENJAMIN CLARK, Mayor

Some Quirky
Chronicles of Yore

SELECTED DISPATCHES PLUCKED FROM FREDERICKSBURG'S
HISTORIC NEWSPAPERS

Fredericksburg's historic newspapers are invaluable sources of information for researchers, genealogists and people interested in history, especially as it was experienced, perceived and reported in this corner of the world.

They also contain an ample supply of very peculiar stories. When using the microfilmed newspapers at Central Rappahannock Regional Library headquarters' Virginiana room, I often get sidetracked by interesting or strange items having nothing to do with the subject I am researching. But I love these distractions, even though they cause me to lose focus on my topic and to waste a lot of time.

When I catch sight of something strange in those distant pages, I am helpless to resist. My curiosity seduced, I am drawn to some freakish item, sometimes captured in a nano-glimpse from the hazy outskirts of peripheral vision. Like Alice descending the rabbit hole, I follow the words, chronicled in evaporated time, to read it all. I need to scrutinize and savor yet another piece of evidence supporting the assertion that life is just plain weird, and always has been.

AN AMAZING EEL

For instance, check out this endearing story of a boy and his overachieving anguilliform. It will leave you eel-ated. The article was taken from the *Philadelphia Times* and reprinted in the *Free Lance* on January 27, 1885:

> *Greensburg, N.Y., is excited just now over Billy Benson's trained eel. Billy is the sixteen-year-old son of farmer Benson. He has been a famous eel catcher for years.*

He made up his mind some time ago that an eel could be trained. He spared the life of one he caught and took it home, putting it in a box with a glass over it. Billy fed it from his own hand. Gradually the eel took a liking to the boy. It would wind its way around the lad's arm and rub its head gently over his sleeve. Then it got so it would come out of the box and coil itself at Billy's feet and go to sleep. Then it learned to follow the boy around, glided up stairs after him, and took to sleeping on the pillow beside him.

Billy named the eel Faithful. In a short while the eel knew its name. So thoroughly educated has it become that it goes all over the farm with the boy, and keeps right along side when he walks at a fast pace. But the funniest thing the eel does is to go fishing with Billy.

It will lie on a log or in a little pond of water and watch the lad haul in any number of other eels and kill them. It never makes any attempt to get into the river. It is moreover a cannibalistic eel and is very fond of small portions of eels' meat which Billy cuts up with his jack knife.

The neighbors go daily to the Benson farm to watch the eel. Many of them wonder how the eel manages to live out of water. There is plenty of water however in Faithful's box so that he is in his native element most of the time.

"SLEEP HATH ITS OWN WORLD..."

"Sleep hath its own world, and a wide realm of wild reality." These words from the English poet Lord Byron seem relevant to the following little dispatch from the *Alexandria Gazette*, via the *Virginia Herald*, published on July 2, 1868:

Mr. E.T.A., who is now on a visit to this city, states that one day last week, while Mr. Mathew W. Rowiston, who resides near Berry's Ferry, in Fauquier County, Va., was dozing with his head reclining upon the side of an open window, a large hawk alighted upon his head, and digging its talons into his flesh, flapped its wings and attempted to rise. Mr. R. being thus suddenly and violently aroused, was of course exceedingly startled, and for a time, as he stated afterwards, he thought the Ku Kluxes had him.

SWAT THAT FLY

From April 24 to May 12, 1913, there were seven reports in the *Free Lance* covering a fly killing campaign organized by Fredericksburg's Civic Betterment Club. The contest was in effect for ten days. Here are some highlights from multiple fly killing reports.

April 24: *The Civic Betterment Club met last Wednesday and listened with great interest to Dr. J.N. Barney's talk on plans for a fly killing campaign.*

Dr. Barney spoke of the housefly as particularly dangerous [as a disease carrier] because of the large numbers in which it appears and the indifference with which most persons accept its presence.

It was decided that the Board of Health and the Civic Betterment Club would conduct a fly killing contest, based on one held in Richmond last year [1912]. The contest would be held from May 1 to May 10 and cash prizes would be offered as follows:

First prize to the one bringing in the largest amount of dead flies, $10; second $5; third and fourth $2.50 each; fifth to tenth $1 each.

This contest is open to any child sixteen years old or under. The same prizes and conditions apply to colored children so this will make twenty prizes to be given.

Representatives from the Civic Betterment Club will measure the dead flies and keep records of those taking part in the contest.

Talks concerning the danger of the housefly and the methods of exterminating it will be made in the schools by some of the physicians of the city.

May 1: *Contestants are reminded that Dr. Barney and representatives of the Civic Betterment Club will be at the Business Men's Association rooms this Saturday for the first measuring of flies. With the first installment of dead flies contestant's names will be entered into the contest.*

Remember that white children bring flies between four and five o'clock and colored between five and six.

This reminder regarding the segregation of fly scorekeeping was published with each update in the news. The kids were kept segregated in all official aspects of the contest. Jim Crow cast a wide net.

May 3: *In view of the generally acknowledged danger of flies to the community in carrying disease, it can easily be seen what value will be such a general extermination of this unwelcome inhabitant of our city.*

While the children are working for these prizes let the grown people also help in raising the standard of cleanliness in Fredericksburg both by killing flies as they appear and by removing from their premises anything that might provide a breeding place for these dangerous pests.

May 12: *Contest closes and the winners are announced. Among the white children first prize went to Frank Hart, 12,650 dead flies. Second prize Edward Carneal, 9,250.*

For the colored children first prize went to Robert Woody, 11,875. Second and third was divided between Rosetta Bass, 8,150 and Raymond Lucas, 8,150.

The contest has closed with a grand total of 189,517 slaughtered flies, but as long as there are any flies in our city let us not rest, but continue to kill them until they are exterminated.

How the fly kills were calculated remains a mystery.

Published September 30, 2006.

A REMARKABLE CASE OF FLOATING AS ACCOMPLISHED BY A COMPOSED VICTORIAN

This dispatch appeared in the *Virginia Herald* on August 27, 1868, courtesy of an unnamed New York correspondent working for the *Chicago Journal*.

A week ago last Thursday night Mr. _____, employed as a clerk at H.B. Claffin and Co., and weighing two hundred and sixty-one pounds, started from the city about 9 o'clock at night to cross over to his home at Hoboken.

The story relates that he slipped off the ferry boat, going unnoticed because of very heavy fog. After swimming a short while he turned over on his back and floated with the tide, unable to see either shore, or get his bearings because of the darkness and fog.

He continued to float down the bay, past Bedloe and Governor's Island, through the Narrows and out to sea. Upon the following morning at half past four a party of New Yorkers in a yacht discovered him off the coast of Staten Island, below the forts, being rapidly borne out to mid-ocean. They let down a small boat and found him in an unconscious condition. The application of some cordials and stimulants soon brought him back to his senses, and he is now back in his establishment performing his accustomed duties.

In describing his experience he said he suffered some from the cold but experienced "greater pains from his inability to relieve the wants of nature."

Contemplating that statement just for a moment can leave one awestruck by the power and hardships imposed by Victorian propriety. Coping with the terror and discomfort of floating out in the middle of New York Harbor in the dead of night you would not think a person would add to that misery by straining to deny nature's call.

The reporter summed up: "This, it seems to me, must be the most remarkable case of floating on record."

I'll say! Our man was in the water for seven hours and was carried nine miles by the tide. He continued to float while unconscious, according to the correspondent.

With a following breeze, he might have made Liverpool by Thanksgiving.

AND YOU THOUGHT SCHLITZ WAS BAD?

"Villainous Milwaukee Whiskey. Five Glasses of it Put a Man to Sleep Forever and for Aye" was the caption for an article republished in the *Free Lance* from the *Milwaukee Journal*, on March 30, 1888.

> *A crowd of men were in John Maechichaefski's saloon at the corner of Greenfield and First Avenue at 9 o'clock in the forenoon* [9:00 a.m.], *when Mr. Hursey entered.*

The conversation wandered to the subject of a man's stomach capacity for the kind of whiskey that was kept in the saloons of that Polish district. Apparently Mr. Hursey's machismo kicked in, and I suspect he was just plain stupid as well.

> *"I bet I can drink five glasses of whiskey in five seconds," said Hursey.*
> *"If you do I'll agree to pay for the stuff," said a bystander, who was apparently acquainted with the deadly character of the stuff.*
> *"I'll take you up," said Hursey, smacking his lips in anticipation.*

A crowd gathered around the bar and the barkeep set out five glasses of the sort usually used for a drink of whiskey. Although the reporter did not specify the size of the glasses he wrote this:

> *A drink of whiskey in the lower district of the south side means something; it means as much as the glass will contain. One, two, three, four five—the liquor gurgled down Hursey's throat as fast as he could empty the glasses. He smiled with satisfaction and the other man threw down the price of the drinks. It wasn't long before Hursey's smile dissolved into a grimace of*

A view of bathing machines at Brighton Front, England, from a postcard dated 1908.
Courtesy of the author.

pain. He said he felt sick and staggered to the nearest chair. His condition worsened fast and finally a doctor was called to the saloon, but it was too late. Hursey died at one o'clock. The coroner was notified and informed about the circumstances. William Hursey was 29-years old, unmarried, and a cigar maker by trade.

To your health!

"MISERIES OF SEA BATHING"

One Mr. Harris, presumably a familiar local in Fredericksburg, related this story to a reporter for the *Virginia Herald*. It was published with the above caption on August 29, 1867. He shared an incident, which he experienced at Pargate, England, a popular seaside resort. Pargate was known for its strong currents and tides.

Before this story continues I have to explain the *bathing machine*, which figures into this narrative. The bathing machine was essential equipment for seaside bathing in the nineteenth century—mostly in the British Empire, and to a lesser extent in the United States and other European countries. The bathing machines were critical to the maintenance and protection of Victorian standards of modesty.

Bathing machines were wooden carts, with walls and a roof, but no windows, which were rolled into and out of the sea, usually pulled by a team of horses. They had steps on the side facing away from shore and some shelves and perhaps a bench inside.

People would change out of their street clothes and into their bathing costume, as swimwear was called, and enter the water without being seen by people on the shore, and most importantly, by the opposite sex. Bathing was legally segregated by gender in England until 1901. Once out with the bathing machine there was sometimes enough privacy to swim in the nude. Women, almost universally, if they did do that, would never admit to it. Instead, they swam clothed in so much fabric it is surprising they didn't drown by the score once soaked. But standards of modesty were not so stridently applied to men. If circumstances allowed, they were more likely to swim in the buff. When the bather was finished, he hoisted a little red flag and the machine would be pulled back to shore by the resort's attendants.

Let us return to Mr. Harris, who suffered a terrible ordeal at Pargate— an incident that was probably not soon forgotten.

Harris told the *Virginia Herald*:

> *I had ordered my vehicle out a great distance, under the impulse of my extreme modesty, and because there were ladies on the beach. I was swimming lazily around the pier head when I suddenly felt myself drifting shoreward. I struggled to regain the [bathing] machine, but the current—the current I had heard so much of—was too much for me. I was not afraid of drowning, for I could keep myself afloat well enough; but worse than death by drowning threatened me; I was being gradually borne, in spite of my efforts, directly down upon the esplanade! I felt myself blushing from head to foot—tingling I may say from top to toe—and the water getting shallower every moment. I dared not turn my face to shore but raised my voice as well as I could.*

Of course Harris was swimming naked.

> *"Ladies!" I said, "the current is carrying me to you feet, upon my word I cannot help it—upon my word I can't—and I shall be on dry land in a couple of minutes. I shall have to run along the beach."* And so he desperately warned them. *"I shall have to run nearly a hundred yards before I can regain my bathing machine."* When I said this I thought they would be off, but I saw they were still there, about four and twenty of them, and I heard the sound of suppressed laughter.
>
> *"Ladies!" I began—and now I wished I might be a sand eel to the end of my days rather than what I was—"ladies don't look in this direction; it is only the cur-cur."*

At this point Harris picked up a mouthful of sand and found himself just ankle deep in the water. That evening, according to Harris, the *Pargate Star* published a special edition devoted to the event.

> *DISGRACEFUL OUTRAGE! We regret to say that the esplanade at Pargate, was made the scene, at mid-day, of a flagrant outrage, the perpetrator of which, we trust, the police will make every effort to secure.*

Apparently Mr. Harris was able to slip out of town and eventually return to Fredericksburg, where he shared his story through the city's principal newspaper. And that is a good thing.

Published March 24, 2007.

Bibliography

THE LITTLE CASTLE

Carr, Myrtle. Interview by author. July 1998. Spotsylvania, VA. Notes in author's file.
Rodgers, Grover. Interview by author. July 1998. Spotsylvania, VA. Notes in author's file.
Spotsylvania County Deed Books 124, 136, 160.

THE JAIL OF THE COUNTY

Bosworth, Frank Maling, III. "An Architecture of Authority: The Jail/ Sheriffs Residences of Northwest Ohio, 1867–1902." PhD diss., Virginia Polytechnic Institute and State University, 1995.
Bruce, Philip Alexander. *Institutional History of Virginia* Vol. 1. New York and London: Knickerbocker Press, 1910, p. 633–646.
Daily Star, February 7, 1913; June 27, 1913; April 2, 1913.
Spotsylvania Citizen, August 31, 1978.
Spotsylvania County Deed Book SS, p. 269.
Spotsylvania County Jail Reports, loose papers Fredericksburg and Spotsylvania Circuit Courts, October 7, 1823; May 24, 1827; August 1, 1853.
Spotsylvania County Order Books, 1838–1843, 1849–1858, 1871–1882.
Virginia Acts of the Assembly, 1849.
Virginia Herald, August 11, 1853; March 8, 1855; April 7, 1858; May 6, 1867.
Virginia Star, February 13, 1884.

A Life of Public Service

Daily Star, February 21, 1900; January 5, 1906; January 25, 1912; April 16, 1912.

Free Lance-Star, May 25, 1944.

Spotsylvania County Deed Books AK, AZ.

Spotsylvania County Land Books 1903, 1909.

Spotsylvania County Order Book 1871–1882.

Spotsylvania County Will Book FC.

Virginia Star, May 28, 1879; May 30, 1883; February 13, 1884.

It's Good for What Ails Ya

Blanton, Wyndom B., MD. *Medicine in the Nineteenth Century.* Richmond: Garrett and Mussie, 1933.

Hand, Wayland D., ed. *American Folk Medicine.* Berkley: University of California Press, 1976.

Kirshtien, C.A. Interview by May Swensen. September 19, 1938. Transcript, Federal Writers' Project, Library of Congress, Washington, D.C.

Naylor, William D. Interview by Earl Bowman. September 19, 1939. Federal Writers' Project, Library of Congress, Washington, D.C.

Numbers, Ronald L., and Todd Savitt, eds. *Science and Medicine in the Old South.* Baton Rouge: Louisiana State University Press, 1989, pp. 276–278, 352–353.

Various People in Spotsylvania County. Interviews by John Tackett Goolrick, 1938–1941. Transcript, WPA Life Histories, Library of Virginia.

Virginia Herald, June 18, 1836; June 9, 1858; January 2, 1871; January 5, 1871; February 20, 1871; January 16, 1871; June 15, 1871; June 29, 1871; September 4, 1871; April 18, 1872; December 22, 1873; May 15, 1873; June 1, 1873; May 11, 1874; April 19, 1875; August 7, 1876; September 14, 1876.

Eldorado Fever

Baron, Bob A. *Gold Mines of Fauquier County.* Berryville: Virginia Book Co., 1977.

Fredericksburg Ledger, April 19, 1870; June 21, 1872.

Fredericksburg News, September 27, 1875; December 6, 1875.

Fredericksburg Star, March 13, 1886; June 2, 1886; July 16, 1887; March 10, 1891.

Free Lance-Star, September 2, 1926; October 18, 1927.

Gaines, William H., Jr. "Piedmont Bonanza." *Virginia Cavalcade* 16, no. 4 (1967).

Knapp, Richard F., and Brent D. Glass. *Gold Mining in North Carolina*. Raleigh: Division of Archives and History North Carolina Department of Cultural resources, 1999, pp. 12, 24, 97.

Spotsylvania County Deed Books V, Z, BB, KK, LL.

Sweet, Palmer C., and David Trimble. "Virginia Gold Resource Data," pub. 45. Charlottesville: Virginia Division of Mineral Resources, 1983.

Virginia Herald, June 20, 1829; May 12, 1830; June 9, 1830; September 15, 1830; March 16, 1831; May 14, 1831; March 27, 1833; December 18, 1833; December 21, 1833; October 4, 1834; November 26, 1834; July 4, 1835; July 1, 1867; May 10, 1869.

WHOLE LOTTA SHEDS GOIN' ON

Dobson, Dora. Interview by author. May 6, 2000. Spotsylvania, VA. Notes in author's file.

Free Lance-Star, May 6, 1935.

Sacra, Sue. Interview by author. May 6, 2000. Spotsylvania, VA. Notes in author's file.

A COMMUNITY FOR LEARNING

Broadside. "Education During the Year 1812." October 10, 1811. Virginia Historical Society.

Holloday, John. Common Place Book. January 9, 1824. Virginia Historical Society.

Lewis, John. Common Place Book. November 1813–February 1819.

Lovett, H.M. Belle Air and Llangollen Papers, Virginia Historical Society.

Mutual Assurance Company insurance policy. February 1816. Llangollen dwelling house.

Richmond Inquiror, September 18, 1826.

Smith, Ethel M. "The Llangollen School for Boys Spotsylvania County, Virginia, 1814–1832," *The Magazine of Virginia Geneaology* 22, 1 (February 1984).

Snow, Charles Melvin. "Educational Trends in Spotsylvania County, 1721–1957. PhD diss., Los Angeles University, 1957.

Virginia Herald, September 8, 1819; December 21, 1825; July 7, 1832; June 15, 1836.

Virginia Historic Landmarks Commission. October 1971. Architectural Survey Form.

HELLO! HELLO!

Council Minutes 1871–1896, City of Fredericksburg Virginia; Council Minutes 1906–1910, vol. 17; Council minutes beginning March 1, 1910, vol. 18; Council Minutes Commencing September 1, 1913, vol. 19; Council Minutes commencing June 1, 1915, vol. 20.

Daily Star, May 17, 1895; September 28, 1895; April 20, 1896; February 22, 1897; July 28, 1897; July 30, 1897; July 2, 1898; February 21, 1900; June 1, 1900; May 15, 1902; February 6, 1903; September 10, 1903; October 8, 1903; October 26, 1903; December 15, 1903; January 2, 1904; March 18, 1904; October 26, 1904; November 30, 1907; July 13, 1909; May 5, 1911; August 14, 1911.

Fredericksburg Star, May 11, 1889.

Free Lance, March 27, 1891; March 28, 1891; February 19, 1895; March 19, 1895; April 12, 1895; April 30, 1895; May 7, 1895; May 17, 1895; September 20, 1895; October 1, 1895; June 1, 1897; July 31, 1897; April 29, 1899; February 22, 1900.

Milestones in AT&T History. http://www.att.com, 2004.

Quinn, S.J. *The History of the City of Fredericksburg.* Richmond: Hermitage Press, 1908, p. 179.

Sanborn Fire Insurance maps. City of Fredericksburg, 1891–1927.

Virginia Star, April 21, 1877.

VOODOO AND CONJURATION

Bodin, Ron. *Voodoo Past and Present.* Lafayette, LA: University of Southwestern Louisiana, 1990, pp. 13–15, 72, 92.

Martin, Dr. John T. (voodoo priest). Interview by author. November 2005. New Orleans, Louisiana. Notes in author's file.

Metraux, Alfred, and Hugo Charteris, trans. *Voodoo in Haiti.* New York: Schoken Books, 1959.

Nickel, Joe. "Investigative Files: Voodoo in New Orleans." *Skeptical Inquirer.* January 2002. http://www.csicop.org.

Perdue, Charles L., Jr., Thomas E. Barden and Robert K. Phillips, eds. *Weevils in the Wheat.* Charlottesville: University Press of Virginia, 1976, pp. 244, 263, 267, 278, 310.

Petition of Peter Hansbrough of the County of Stafford, petition in regard to a slave, 1773. *Virginia Historical Magazine*, Miscellaneous Documents Colonial and State, 1910, vol. 18, 394.

Pucket, Newbell Miles, PhD. *Folk Beliefs of the Southern Negro*. Chapel Hill: University North Carolina Press, 1926, pp. 177, 242, 286, 310.

The Pledge and the Brotherhood

By-Laws Mount Hermon Division no. 348, Spotsylvania County. Fredericksburg, VA: J. White, 1850[?], p. 6–16. Virginia Historical Society, Richmond.

Evans, Thomas J. *A digest of the resolutions and decisions of the National Division of the Sons of Temperance of the United States, and of the Grand Division of Virginia, embracing a brief history of the origin, progress and present attainment of the order.* Richmond: H.K. Ellyson, 1847.

Ferm, Vergilius, ed. *An Encyclopedia of Religion*. See "Temperance Movement." New York: Philosophical Library, Inc., 1945.

Fredericksburg News, September 4, 1849; November 30, 1849; July 18, 1853.

Harris, Jeremiah. Diary 1851–1860. Manuscripts, 52–53, 63–64. Virginia Historical Society, Richmond.

Holloday, Waller. Minute Book, Sons of Temperance. Mt. Hermon Division. September 28, 1850. Virginia Historical Society, Richmond.

Martin, Alexander. *Prize Essay on the Principals and Operations of the Order of the Sons of Temperance* 2d ed. Richmond: H.K. Ellyson, 1851. Virginia Historical Society, Richmond.

Sons of Temperance North America. *Funeral Ceremony for Order of Sons of Temperance*. Richmond: H.K. Ellyson, 1855[?].

"The Temperance Reform." *The Virginia Historical Register* 3 (1850): 152–157.

Virginia Herald, April 16, 1863.

Weekly Advertiser, March 5, 1853; May 7, 1853; January 7, 1860.

"Oh What a Luxury!"

Daily Star, December 6, 1905; December 15, 1905; December 16, 1905; December 18, 1905; December 22, 1905; December 23, 1905; December 26, 1905; December 30, 1905.

Free Lance, November 25, 1905; December 2, 1905; December 7, 1905; December 9, 1905; December 14, 1905; December 16, 1905; December 18, 1905; December 19, 1905; December 23, 1905; December 26, 1905; December 28, 1905; December 30, 1905.

ON THE ROAD

Council Minutes, City of Fredericksburg, 1906–1910, vol 17, Beginning March 1, 1910, vol. 18; Council Minutes Commencing September 1, 1913, vol. 19; Commencing September 1, 1913, vol. 19, 18.

Daily Star, April 5, 1907; April 16, 1907; March 7, 1908; March 9, 1908; May 5, 1910; May 6, 1910; May 4, 1911; July 1913; September 19, 1913.

Fredericksburg City Directory, 1919, 1921.

Sanborn Fire Insurance Maps. City of Fredericksburg, 1907, 1912, 1919.

Virginia Acts of the Assembly, 1906, p. 35.

Virginia Acts of the Assembly, 1916, pp. 525–529.

Warsaw (Virginia) Northern Neck News, May 8, 1908.

WHEN RUBBER MET CINEMA

Bettis, John, and Pamelia Bettis. Interview by author. October 14, 2006. Spotsylvania, VA. Notes in author's file.

Drive-ins of Virginia. http://www.driveinmovie.com/VA. Accessed August 31, 2006.

Free Lance-Star, December 1, 1950; April 3, 1951; April 21, 1951; August 21, 1956.

IMDb: Earths Biggest Movie Database. *Wives Beware*, 1932. http://www.imdb.com. Accessed October 13, 2006.

Mann, Jim. Telephone interview by author. October 2006. Fredericksburg, VA. Notes in author's file.

Pitts, B.T. Clippings File. *Free Lance-Star.* Fredericksburg,VA.

Richmond News Leader, March 29, 1956.

U.S. Bureau of the Census. *Statistical Abstract of the United States*. 1951.

POLICING THE CORPORATION

Campbell, T.E. *Colonial Caroline: A History of Caroline County, Virginia.* Richmond: Dietz Press, 1954, pp. 361–363.

Council Minutes City of Fredericksburg, 1782–1801, 1801–1829, 1829–1851.

Fredericksburg District Court Order Book B 1794–1798.

Fredericksburg News, March 31, 1856.

Henning, William Waller, ed. *Virginia Statutes at Large.* Vol. 10 "Acts of the Assembly 1781." Richmond: George Cochran, 1822.

Hustings Court Order Book B 1782–1787; Book C 1787–1800.

Mayo, Joseph. *A Guide to Magistrates; with practical forms for the discharge of their duties out of court. To which are added precedents for the use of prosecutors, sheriffs, coroners, constables, escheators, clerks, &c.* Richmond: Nash and Woodhouse, 1853, pp. 484, 485.

Miller, Michael T., compiler. *Murder and Mayhem: Criminal Conduct in Old Alexandria Virginia 1749–1900.* Bowie, MD: Heritage Books Inc., 1988, pp. vi–ix.

Political Arena, April 30, 1841; October 22, 1841; July 21, 1846.

U.S. Bureau of the Census. *Heads of Families at the first census of the United States taken in the year 1790: records of the State enumerations 1782–1785, Virginia.* Washington, DC: Government Printing Office, 1907–1908.

Virginia Acts of the Assembly, 1801.

Virginia Acts of the Assembly, 1807, p. 124.

Virginia Acts of the Assembly, 1852, p. 4.

Virginia Acts of the General Assembly, 1792, p. 219.

Virginia Herald, June 19, 1788; July 30, 1789; October 15, 1789; February 25, 1790; July 24, 1790; February 10, 1791; May 3, 1792; July 31, 1793; July 9, 1795; October 3, 1795; July 18, 1800; August 19, 1806.

About the Author

Ted Kamieniak was born in Hollis, Queens, a borough of New York City, and he grew up in New Hyde Park, a nearby Long Island suburb. As a child he was attracted to history and old objects and houses. Once, while exploring a historic abandoned house, he discovered a cache of yellowed, mouse-nibbled newspapers. Many of the papers contained coverage of the First World War. At the bottom of the stacks was a copy of the May 8, 1915 *New York Times* reporting the sinking of the *Lusitania*.

Following high school, Ted spent several years among the Adirondack Mountains of northern New York, where he developed a love of the natural world. In the North Country he attended community college and worked as an intern and freelance writer with the *Adirondack Daily Enterprise* in Saranac Lake. "The Only Daily Published in the Adirondack Park," it proudly proclaims beneath its flag. He wrote drama, television and film reviews and features about Adirondack history.

After moving to Virginia he earned an undergraduate degree in historic preservation from the University of Mary Washington in Fredericksburg, an accomplishment that strengthened his interests in historical research, writing and cultural resources. Ted had the pleasure of serving on Spotsylvania County's Historic Preservation Commission for several years.

He is a freelance writer who contributes to the *Free Lance-Star's Town & County* magazine, and he researches and composes articles relating to local history and a variety of other topics.

He enjoys collecting and reading books, bass fishing, canoeing or tubing the Rappahannock River with his kids, hiking, upland bird hunting in the mountains and hollows of western Virginia and collecting and studying odd bits of material culture. He also likes visiting historic sites and investigating vernacular architecture and old homesteads. Gardening and watching wildlife are favored pastimes as well.

He lives in Spotsylvania County with his wife Cindy, his mother Jenny and his son Jake, and he has a daughter, Eva, who is away at college. Two bichon frisés and three parrots round out the household.